Ancient Law of Environment

Ancient Law of Environment

Dr. R.G. Chaturvedi
Ph. D., D. Litt.
Advocate

Universal
Law Publishing Co. Pvt. Ltd.
NEW DELHI - INDIA

2010 Edition

ISBN : 978-81-7534-962-9

Published by
UNIVERSAL LAW PUBLISHING CO. PVT. LTD.
C-FF-1A, Dilkhush Industrial Estate,
(Near Azadpur Metro Station) G.T. Karnal Road,
Delhi-110 033
Tel : 011-27438103, 27215334, 42381334
Fax : 011-27458529
E-mail *(For sales inquiries)* : sales@unilawbooks.com
E-mail *(For editorial inquiries)* : edit@unilawbooks.com
Website : www.unilawbooks.com

Recommended citation: *Ancient Law of Environment,* Dr. R.G. Chaturvedi (New Delhi: Universal Law Publishing Co. Pvt. Ltd., 2010)

Computer Typeset at Aesthetic & *Printed* at Vishal Binding House, NOIDA.

PROLOGUE

Environment is exoteric name of cosmos. Being constituent of the cosmos, environment is integument of the cosmos and is perennially governed by cosmic laws. The environmental legislation takes, as it can, an isolated fragmentary and ephemeral view of the environment and the endeavour to remedy the environmental malady amounts to simulating the administering of sedative pills to cure spiritual ills. The global conferences and local seminars on these terse subjects are naturally oblivious to cosmic truths, and they have not secured any positive advantage to set the things right.

Environment is not physics but metaphysics. It is not a subject but a science. It is not physiography but cosmography, and there is no authority on cosmography other than word of the Veda. In the Vedic law, the cosmocraft is not material phenomenon but a spiritual pageant. In the self-conscious universe, the environment feels and wills, acts and reacts. It is benevolent only in *status quo* but is prone to be malevolent if aggrieved. The evils rampant in the society and a global criminality in practice, has disintegrated the spirituality of men. This spiritual damage is damage of the cosmic spirit and the environment reacts in retaliation rather then its redemption. The spirit in man is mini-cosmos and anything occurring to man pollutes the environment.

The spiritual dimensions of environmental ethics are based on science of *Yajna,* which has now sunk into remissness. This is open hostility to environment but causes are being investigated elsewhere. The environment is an organic whole. The compass and expanse of environment are the fundamentals of this study.

The Darwinian theory of origin of species is more fiction then fact. In the Vedic cosmology the tree of life has its roots above and has its twigs downward. The life on earth has come from the *Rishis* and the *Pitras* which is irrefutable cosmic science. The other two theories laid by Herbert Spencer and Henry Bergson, are corollaries to the Darwinian phantasy.

The temporal life, or the life incarnate is the culmination of the life principle throughout infused in the cosmos with the result that life patterns or forms, or designs of life, are first projected in the ethereal space. The cosmic space, thus, provides for centres of creative power for every root or parent life patterns of the host of forms of botanical or zoological life; and each pattern is a generalized design worked out by the cosmic designer. These centres contain a specific germ or spark of life, and can be conceived as the cosmic mason or manufactor, at work like a smith on his bellows. The bellows represent the cosmic life principle.

There is law which keeps this cosmofactory in action, and that law is the law of *Karma* and rebirth.

The cosmos itself has its life and is liable to dissolve in the same way as a dead body. The cosmos is bound by the collective *karma* of the previous creation, and the collective *karma* of the current term of the cosmos will determine the subsequent creation. The individual self is bound by this immutable cosmic law and determines his life on rebirth on the merit of his actions done in the past life. This is the law of *karma* stated in simplest terms.

The inspiration for this effort is to supply the desideratum in the field of knowledge of environment with a dedication to the spiritual end of the cosmos. The clean conscience in man can alone anticipate a halcyonic environment.

August 2010 **R.G. Chaturvedi**

CONTENTS

CHAPTER 4
FALLACIES OF MODERN EVOLUTIONARY THEORIES

CHAPTER 5
KARMA AND REBIRTH

CHAPTER 6
PATTERNS OF LIFE

CHAPTER 1

ENVIRONMENT: A SPIRITUAL PHENOMENON

SYNOPSIS

1. Spirituality Explained
2. Self as Arbiter of Values
3. Categorical Imperative as Cosmic Intuition
4. Oneness of Nature
5. Environment Operates in Unison with Thought
6. Quantum Theory and Consciousness
7. The Imposing Question

1. Spirituality Explained

The term 'Spirit', in substance, refers to the essence of a thing. Spirituality is different since it combines both ethology and soteriology. 'Spiritualism' is further different, since it refers to a cult adept in communication with departed souls.

Spirituality is not cult but is commonsense since ingrained in the subtlety of soul. A spontaneous deference to some transcendental, unseen power, is domain of religion. On the other hand, a conative conduct or inclination to do or abstain from doing something is the conserved content of the being of man which functions as the impartial spectator around, and operates as immediate imperative within the self, that is, the sinecure sentinel of the autonomy of self. The former is epiphany: latter is ethics, the former is individual intuition; latter is collective command; the former consists in the belief unto a divinity; latter is commitment to a collectanea of exhortations. Viewed from its organizational side, spirituality has, therefore, two components: religion and values. The former denotes faith in particular man whereas the latter connotes the collective conscience of humanity viewed as the perpetual repository of perennial values, transcending time and tide of temporal or social vicissitudes.

The belief in God, too, particularly in religions not committed to a personal or creator God, finally recedes to the fabric of faith, adopted, followed or borrowed. Likewise, the esoteric spectrum of values is found finally reduced to pragmatic notions of likes and dislikes.

I value the things I reflexively like, and the things I dislike, I do not value, yet the 'I' as the subject is not my individual ego but the vestige of an altruistic universal 'I'ness, sharing the common surveillance of human empathy, so that the expression "I like" is elevated to the universal liking of 'I', 'you' and 'he'.

Likes and dislikes, as positive content of values, may, hence, be illustrated in terms of the individual self as well as of the social ethos.

The former is matter of need and choice, the latter is that of consciousness which comprises the properly so called conscientious values, for which there is no choice but the impulsion to sublimely subdue.

The likes and dislikes emanate from the self and the self alone is the arbiter of values, at least in mundane matters, but the position is different in relation to conscientious values, pure and simple.

2. Self as Arbiter of Values

Sage *Yajnyavalkaya,* as an anecdote in the *Brihadaranyak Upnishad*[1] goes, decided on the eve of his

1. 2/4/5.

renunciation, to settle an equitable division of his assets between his two consorts. The Sage made it specific that he owned two types of assets – one household things, and the other, his knowledge: and each of them could choose. The Sage extended the first option to his junior wife, and she being a lady from domestic moorings, readily opted for the household, with the result that the secret asset of higher knowledge eventually fell to the share of the senior legatee.

Insinuating the propriety of choice for transitory and perishable things, the senior dame posed a question as to what these mundane things could be valued for.

The considered reply of the Sage was illustrative as well as exhaustive. Evincing from individual relations, the Sage said that the husband is not dear for the sake of the husband, nor is the son dear for the sake of the son, but either is dear for the sake of the self, and so is the case of any limb or organ of the body or any other relation or association of the self which alone is the sanctuary of all affections and endearments.

The proposition can stand far truer in the modern contexts, where the husband can be deserted or divorced, and a son can be condemned or disowned, for any misdemeanor, and bereft of their association with the self, both cease to be dear to the self. Therefore, the idea of the self itself is fragmentary without reference to the fullness of reality.

In the context of the whole, there are ascensions and descentions. From down upwards, the man proceeds to expand his horizon to become the universe. From above downwards, the universe is reduced to the individual. Man as part of the universe, comes down to be member of the society and recedes to a point where he is his own self. The process oscillates from a larger whole to the smaller and *vice versa*. Even the smallest whole represents a system of its own. Left alone, the man is a universe in miniature. He has a system within which he regulates his outer life.

The outer behavior of man is the manifestation of his inner self. He creates a world to live in and attempts to shape it to his inner ideal. The evidence is an account given by Alexander Serventes in his *Robinson Crusoe*, thrown, in a shipwreck, on a forlorn Island. From oddments of the shipwreck, he manufactured implements, and, in course of time, he expanded his universe, collected a large number of goods and chattel; possessed a host of animals and pets.

Each man has to do it, whether in a lone island or in a multitudinous society. He gradually expands the horizon of his universe and realizes it in the outer world. He acquires land and erects a dwelling; settles a family and begets children; affords food and hoards money; collects goods and accumulates chattel; makes friends and creates relations. It then, becomes difficult to dissociate his self from his little world. He has a fetish for his chattel and attachment with his belongings. He becomes one with his world, identifying his goods, chattel or relations with himself. The objects and relations are parts of his own person. It is through them that he asserts and expresses his self. His title to each of them is unquestionable. They are his, because he claims them in and against the whole world. Each of them has value to him because he has a right to it. Here, the corpus of his rights or relations is the *terra firma* of his values and it is in these values that his spirituality is outsighted and which, as a matter of fact, is his secondary spirituality different from the primary or the insighted spirituality which is absolute and independent of his exterior relations and outward rights.

Thus, a house is a value to the one who has a right to dwell therein. A bread or meat is of value to him who has a right to taste the stuff. The objects and chattel are good to him who has a right to their use or possession. A house to the destitute may be necessary but is good to him when given to live in. A bread or meat is essential to the hungry but good only when given to eat. The objects and chattel are no good to one denied the right to posses and use them.

A right is merely the dominating relation of a man with the thing or object of his necessity; and a relation is one which creates a right and a corresponding duty in the mutual inter-currents of that relation; and the good consists in the absence of obstruction to, or the usurpation of that thing or relation. A right may, thus, be temporary, permanent or perpetual, in view of the temporary or permanent absence of such obstruction or usurpation. The spirituality on this plane is, therefore, evanescent, lasting so long as the right or the relation lasts and is liable to suffer change or decay in the course of progression of the self. The right and relations being part of the man's being, is the essence of his personality, and the spirituality, having the prescience of catholicity, is different as composing the subtlety of the soul. Right from birth to death, the self, though an integrated whole, is not throughout the same self.

In early childhood, the value concept concentrates on objects of rudimentary attachment, like mother, milk, playthings and playmates, replaced in adolescence by friendship, company and career, developing, later in youth into status, stability and settlement, and finally, in the advanced age, a sense of detachment draws the subject to a search for sublimation and salvation, and there may be thousands of incidents surrounding each step in the gradual progression of the self.

The growth of the self discovers values in a liberal schedule and lofty perspective, vivifying those in academic attainments, social security, political stability and economic prosperity; and for all such values, the self has taken to mighty modes of its expansion. Starting from the self as a concentric unit, and aspiring yet to identify with the universal human fraternity, the human reason is restive to discover the values that are still unattained as well as to drop those that have turned anachronistic. Humanity is vastly busy in the generation and regeneration of values.

In proportion to the expanse of the self in the outer universe, the values have to widen their peripheries. A family or a club, a class or the community, a nation or the Commonwealth of Nations, are each an expansion of the self in a graduated hierarchy. The self identifies with each in relation to the value motivating most at the given moment. In each case, the self assumes new dimensions and aspires further for newer or higher dimensions. The landing on the Moon or the assault on the Mars, are pure endeavours towards stages for oneness with the infinite: and this oneness with the cosmic purpose is the core of spirituality.

Each new dimension of the self is a stage of hierarchy in the schematized oneness, placing the self in its possible amplitudes. The innate eagerness of the self widening its vigour and sphere and seeking to culminate in the final oneness of the infinite, would only be a spiritual event difficult to regulate but definite to realize. In this state alone, the self reposes in spirituality and rests in peace; and it is in this state that values attain their apex, and ethics becomes metaphysics, or, in other words, righteousness becomes religion.

A vast difference is noticeable between mundane values and the really conscientious or spiritual values. In relation to the former, the self is an active arbiter; in case of the latter, the self is passive abider. The mundane values are conative and relative. The conscientious ones are emotive and absolute. On the plane of conscientious values, the self feels at par with all others, at times, at par with every creature, and acts as a trustee of the truth and tenet of those values. The mundane values operate in a given ambience and are subject to social reforms or temporal upheavals, extending upto statutory interventions. The conscientious part of values, being the real content of spirituality stands intact, immutable and inviolate; and there can be a law to punish its breach, but no law is needed to declare it as binding.

The mundane values, dwelling in the domain of rights and relations are matters of particularity. The universe of a man's rights or relations is limited, and he can enlarge them in a given sphere. No one can be owner of all the wealth in the world and, even in his aspiration to have more, he has to be content with what he possesses. A man's relations with his chattel is based on the principle of rights, though not on basis of principle of righteousness, and on the principle of general conditions and categories of rights, each owner, on the same enology, has a claim, to the same extent in relations to his own chattel.

Once the sphere of vision is enlarged and the human rights or relations are viewed in the perspective of the humanity, the question of 'I' and 'My', of 'he' and 'his' becomes secondary and less significant. What comes of primary and of first significance, is not the question of 'he' and 'his chattel' in particular but of 'chattels' and the 'owners' in general. The category of 'rights' and 'owners' is universalized. A particular house, a particular meal or a particular chattel, assumes a meaning as the general right to shelter, to food, and to property, and a machinery, in general interest, like the State and the law, may be evolved to keep intact these rights: and it is clear that the State or the law is not the source of these rights; **State and law are only sanctions on sanctity of rights.** The rights emanate from the sense of ego in the self and a political order is needed to keep them secure.

In asserting his right, a particular man wields his particular will. When the same will is discovered in relations to the rights all men, the particular will becomes the universal will; and since this will comes from within the self, as constituent of the cosmos, it is cosmic will, because the natural will in the self can only be the will of nature. **The nature in man is part of nature at large.** Man being product of nature, the source of all his faculties of knowing, willing and feeling, like all his physical frame, can only be the manifestations in him of the vast nature in the cosmos.

This will of nature, as is expressed in the *Manual* of Epictetus, is discovered in those matters on which there can be no difference of opinion. So when another man's wine cup is broken, it is easy to say: "Such things must happen", but when one's own cup is broken, he ought to behave in the same way when his neighbor's was broken; and when this principle is applied on higher matters, one has to submit to a discipline not imposed from outside but inspired from inside, as **Jesus Christ** said, in the *Sermon on the Mount*, that:

> "Judge not that ye be not Judged. For when what judgment ye judge, ye shall be judged; and with what measure ye mete, it shall be measured to you again."

So when the measure is that no one's wine cup be broken, the taboo is not invented by Epictetus. The taboo existed all along the line of humanity and Epictetus only insighted it. The moral in man is seen writ large on humanity, and it is this way that righteous conduct becomes religion and taboos are set in scriptures like the *Ten Commandments* in the *Holy Bible,* as they are:

Thou shalt not kill;

Thou shalt not commit adultery;

Thou shalt not steal;

Thou shalt not bear false witness against thy neighbour;

Thou shalt not covet thy neighbour's house;

Thou shalt not covet thy neighbour's wife, nor his man-servant nor his maid-servant nor his ox, nor his ass, nor anything that is thy neighbour's;

These or other commandments are not reared by but only registered in the Bible as categorical imperatives which are ingrained in the conscience even of the first man, *Adam* or *Manu* as be conceived in different scriptures. **The categorical imperative in the conscience is, in effect, built upon cosmic intuition.**

3. Categorical Imperative as Cosmic Intuition

In his *Foundations of Metaphysic of Morals,* **Immanuel Kant** conceived the human being as an embodiment of the free will. The human good consists in the freedom of will. The two maxims that the individual ought to do a thing because he can, and that he can, because he ought, can be transposed one for the other.

Freedom of will is simple right of self-determination. There is nothing more dreadful to Kant than that the will of man be subordinated to that of another. The right of man to do something according to his will is the basis of human destiny. The proposition is warm with Rousseau's influence who opened his *Social Contract* with the aphorism that *man is born free yet he is everywhere in chains.* Man is free but the chains which bind him, have their roots in reason.

Freedom is not self contradiction. The free will is, therefore, bound to be a self-consistent will. Kant's free actions, similar to good activities viewed by **Aristotle**, in his *Nicomachean Ethics*, are based on a rational element in soul.

The metaphysics of Aristotle was committed to the principle of *universals*. Kant's theory of law stands on the universal character of law and Kant's improvement consists in universalizing the rational basis of law. Moral virtue emanates from reason. If everything in nature acts according to laws, the nature acts according to reason; and in acting according to reason, the nature is moral, out and out, and it is this difference between cosmic and human natures that whereas cosmic nature cannot act contrary to reason, man is free to act contrary to reason. **The nature has no freedom to defy its law; man is free to defy laws and to denounce even dictates of reason.**

The real call of nature need not be referred to an end beyond itself. It is wrong to make hypothetical statements and say that one ought to do this or that if he should attain this or that objective. It has to be simply done because it is a command of the reason and not a whim of the will. It is to be done for its own sake, because it is the dictate of one's reason. The call is imperative, since it has, behind it, the ideation of reason, and such dictate has to be adhered to not simply here or there or now or then, but has to be obeyed in all times and at all places. It is of unexceptionable category and since it is unexceptionable, it is categorical, because it is not a subjective choice but an objective compulsion. Being objective, it is an end in itself. It is duty for duty's sake, as the *Bhagwadgita*[1] acclaims that all rights are confined

1. 2/47.

to the doing of duties. The individual being an embodiment of this imperative, is an end in himself.

To breach or violate what is categorical, it to lead to contradictions. If the breach is universalized, the breach itself becomes impossible. To abstain from stealing is an imperative. To universalize the violation of this imperative is to repudiate the institution of private property itself. If everybody were allowed to steal with impunity, there would be no property, worth the name, to steal, and this is self-contradiction. If everybody could break a promise, a promise would betray and degenerate into a lie, which is, again, self-contradictory.

In application to oneself, the Kantian maxim is: *Act if the maxim of your action were to become through your will a general law*. In application to others, the maxim is: *Act only according to a maxim by which you can at the same time will that it shall become a general law*. Governed by the categorical imperative, the man is an end in himself, and the community, a kingdom or commonwealth of ends. To be rational is to be amenable to all and maintain the law.

The rational foundation of law need not be based on reciprocity of behavior. It springs from the inner co-ordination of rival instincts giving rise to conflicting motives. The categorical imperative is the freedom to rule oneself and is the result of a pre-established harmony, that is, the uniformity of mind in one and all; and **there is no other way to define spirituality than this uniformity of operations of mind in one and all**. This uniformity comes from an inner intuition, because it is operation of the cosmic mind; and had there been no cosmic mind, there could never be uniformity in the operation of one and all minds. If fire is to warm or water is to wet, to one and all, and if a thorn pricks one and all alike, the sensation is cosmic and the individual shares that experience when exposed to that situation without any innovation of his own. What operates instinctively is only cosmic instinct manifest in all without distinction or discrimination. It is on this basis that one likes to do to others what he likes others to do to him. In doing what one does not like others to do to him, or in avoiding what one likes to do, is to be at war with oneself. In choosing to stab *Caesar* which he ought not, is aptly described by *Shakespeare*, in his *Julius Caesar*, as *Brutus at war with himself*. The thief in stealing and the traitor in his treachery, is always at war with himself since he never likes that others should steal from or commit treachery to him. The thief and the traitor, both know, that they are violating a pre-established harmony.

In his treatise on *Two sources of Morality and Religion* **Henry Bergson** wondered *What a childhood it would have been if everybody was allowed to do as he pleased*, but an obstruction was soon discovered in the authority of parents and teachers, and the would-be parents had received it from their own teachers or parents, and so on, in the unfathomable preterite past, so as to assign its origin to some preterhuman source. Not to do as one pleases, hence, stays as an injunction instilled in the nature of man, and in doing contrary to that, the doer palpably acts contrary to his spirit and in violation of his nature. It is the nature at large which has injected this injunctive theme in the nature of man, and there is no alternative but to concede to this pre-vision.

The self commands the other selves to an agreed course of conduct for his own sake. It is for his own safety that each isolated self becomes juxtaposed in a community of selves like the component cells of an organism so that submission to a standard for others is imposed on the self as of necessity. The component cell of an organism, says **Bergson**, in the opening chapter of his above treatise, *on becoming momentarily conscious, would* *barely have outlived the wish to emancipate itself when it would be recaptured by necessity.* The general discipline is, thus, preserved by individual obligations obtaining between concrete personalies of 'I' and 'you'.

A distinct spirit is inculcated for conceiving specifically this kind of situation in a hierarchical structure of contextual levels. **Bertrand Russell**, referred to in the *Self Aware Universe,* by **Amit Goswami** with **Richard E. Reed** and **Maggie Goswami**, named this spirit as *the theory of logical types,* with the idea thereunder that a set consisting of members of the set is of a higher logical type than the members themselves because it is the set which defines the context for thinking about the members. **Plato's** theory of ideas is only a dedication to this higher context of spirituality, because the name of a thing, which depicts the class of those things, *Man, Cow, Chair, Table,* and so for all common nouns, is of a higher logical type than the thing itself which is that thing so long as it conforms or approximates to that idea. Such idea being immortal or eternal, there is an eternal idea behind each spiritual connotation, and the individual self, by necessity of nature, conforms to that idea. The man is committed to that idea by force of nature, because even the worst of the sinner would never advise his own kins to sin. This commitment is imperative, and the imperative is a cosmic phenomenon: because it comes from eternity; and the individual is born with an imprint thereof in him.

Aristotle's faith in this spirituality appears in the same tone of his theory of *universals* and *particulars.*

The particular is only the manifested objectivity of the universal which exists immutable. The individual is to the cosmos as the cells are to the body of an organism. **The imperatives of man and nature are one and uniform.**

The individual simply commands some imperative on others as a representative of the cosmic self since the human nature is only active instrument of that imperative in evidence of oneness of nature.

4. Oneness of Nature

The cosmic nature and the nature in man, are as integral to each other as the cosmic life to lives of creatures in general, and it is this way that culmination of thought in any religion, any ethics or metaphysics, has been towards oneness of the process of life and thought both; and there is no rest until it is realized that the cosmic self and the individual self are one, and the process of being and the affectations of one are automatic affectations of the other, as when a drop of poison in the ocean howsoever innocuous to the mass, is yet a pollution of the whole sea. **Pollution of thought is pollution of nature, defilement of an individual nature is degradation of the cosmic nature**.

Environment and its pollution only register the ideational pollution, and both operate in unison.

5. Environment Operates in Unison with Thought

That man is part of the cosmos, needs no evidence.

The nature is primary name of environment. **Environment is only a compressed and commonsense name of nature.** The nature is a system; environment is process. Nature is cause; environment is instrumentality for that cause to bring effects. Environment exhibits the plan and the interconnection of cause and effect involved in the system.

This belief in the process of oneness is evidenced both in scriptures and science.

So, when one of the *Ten Commandments* in the *Old Testament* ordains- *Thou shall not kill*, the implication is that thou shall not kill (me). The commandment enjoined on one, not to kill another, is simple principle contributing to the utility of life. This is what **Sir E. B. Taylor** maintains in his *Anthropology,* that the tribe makes its law not on an abstract principle that manslaughter is right or wrong, but for its own preservation, and the word *kindness,* as he says, owes its origin to the word *kindred.* In doing against a principle, the doer is temporarily exiled from his own self, and, in his relating back to the principle, he is restored to his self. In the former, as the *Bhagwadgita*[1] says, the self acts as his own enemy whereas in the latter, he becomes self-friendly.

The creaturehood is only particle of the cosmic whole, says, again, the *Gita.*[2] In his *Mysterious Universe,* **Sir James Jeans** has realized the resemblance of the scheme of nature with the mind of a mathematician. **Whitead**, in his *Religion in the Making,* is convinced that this scheme of the universe is revelation of creativity with freedom. **Eddington**, in his *Nature of the Physical World,* testifies that the stuff of the universe is relational and the indeterminacy detected in the course as a whole may be accident but not arbitrariness. It is a widely popular belief held by science that matter is the primary stuff of creation and proposes, instead, that consciousness is the true foundation of all we know and perceive. It is now scientific belief that the quantum waves are only waves of consciousness.

When one integrated phenomenon like the *Prakriti* and the *Purusha,* in the *Samkhya* school of Indian Philosophy, operate in reaction to each other, it is futile to cavil which of them is antecedent and which a

1. 6/5.
2. 15/7.

consequent. **The quantum theory is inert dynamicity; consciousness is sentient beneficiary thereof;** and both operate in tandem with and for each other. The operation is reciprocal.

6. Quantum Theory and Consciousness

Quantum physics says that objects are waves and waves, as is well-known, can exist at two or more places at the same time; and there is no paradox if, practically, the objects are seen only at one place, since what is perceived as object is perceived because of the waves the conglomeration of the atoms and molecules in the object constantly emit; and the case with consciousness, which is the agency registering that emission as a sensible behavior, is not different as when beholding the peak of a mountain, quite from a distance, the consciousness of the peak is always both at the peak and in the psyche. That objects are waves, is only a metaphor for the process of emission of the waves from the object to the percipient self, so that the quantum theory and the theory of consciousness are both intervolved in one and the same phenomenon, and there is no better way to define either.

Defined in the simplest terms, the quantum theory is that atoms and molecules emit or absorb a discrete quanta of energy, and energy can travel only in waves; but since emission or absorption represents the changes of energy, each commensurate to the multiple of a fundamental quantum, what is discrete in this process is really discreet, and since the energy inherent in the atom or the molecules can operate in a sensible way, **the energy is the same thing as consciousness in function.**

Consciousness is defined similarly, in yet simpler terms as the combined activity of intellect and senses; and this combination discernible in the recipience of each sensation of smell, of hearing, sight, touch and taste.

The senses are only instruments of the intellect. The senses register, record and report the impressions they receive from objects, events and action to the intellect. The intellect ratiocinates, classifies and categorises them in its experience. In the case of hearing, the intellect discerns the sonorous from the discordant. In case of seeing, it differentiates between the lovely and the loathsome. In case of touch, it discriminates between soft and hard. In case of taste, it determines the sour, sweet or the pungent. In case of smell, it disposes the fragrant from the stinky. In the network of consciousness, the intellect and the senses are engaged together in any sensible or sensable activity, and even where this consciousness is disengaged from outside object, it is still self-consciousness, content with the experience of the inner stimulations or the silent activities of the self.

This consciousness is not, however a manipulation of the self. The limbs and organs in the body and the intellect, mind and sense in the self, are all endowments of nature. The consciousness in the self is paraphysis of the cosmic consciences in the sense that whereas in the nature at large it is introverted, it is extroverted in the self.

The question, imposing, of course, then, is whether the conscious commissions or omissions of the individual can have any percussion on the nature. **Nature is just metaphysical name of environment, and the environment is exoteric process of the esoteric principle of nature.**

7. The Imposing Question

The man is cosmos in miniature is perennial faith of the **Vedas**. The agencies, commissioned by nature for cosmic function, find and take their corresponding situs and assume their respective function in the human, nay, in any organism. The Sun is the intellect as well as the manifest eye, and the Moon is the mind of the cosmic self, says the *Yajurveda*.[1] The function of the intellect is to lead from nescience to knowledge with its corollary, to lead from darkness to light. **The intellect is plasma of the cerebrum**, known in the *Yoga* cult as the *Sahasrar*, that is, having thousand rungs, and in relation to the knowledge of objects, the intellect functions through the eye. The *Gayatri* hymn, which a Brahmin is expected to recite everyday, is an incantation to the Sun for elevation of the intellect. The affinity of man and mind is well evidenced by the tidal upheaval in the bosom of the ocean and by the bizarre behaviour of the lunatic on the full Moon. The sky, for the word, the air for the touch, the fire for the colour, the water for the taste and the earth for the smell, are sensory apparatus of the cosmic self, as goes the evolutionary theory in the *Samkhya* School of Indian philosophy, not refuted so far by any other philosophy.

Thus, the ingredients which enter into the composition of consciousness at the macro level are the Sun, the Moon and the five elements of sky, air, fire, water and earth. On the micro level, the same become manifest as the intellect, the mind, and the five senses of hearing, touch, sight, taste and smell, and since the latter are only derivatives of the former, the difference only is that whereas the consciousness of the cosmic self is infinite and boundless, that of the individual is finite and bounded. That which is infinite is unmanifest, and can have no choice like the freedom of will. Freedom of will is attribute only of the finite, since choice is another name of limitations. In choosing between 'this' or 'that', the 'this' limits 'that' and *vice versa*. Limitations come from differences. In choosing, for example, between 'white' and 'black' the white and black are both finite and

1. 31/1.

limited in the sense that be it white or black, neither can be red, green, pink or amygdalic. Both are thesis and antithesis to each other, as **Hegel** would support in his two books on *Logic.*

To limit is to contradict which is possible in relative and finite concepts. The Infinite can have no contradictions, and, therefore, no limitations. There can be no limitations in the composite hole. **The nature is not scheming but schematised and though it wills but its will works only one way, without choice of deviation.**

The satanic forces can beguile only the finite but not the Infinite. In the *Genesis,* the Serpent could beguile Eve, but not God, and the annoyance of God was not against beguilement by the Serpent but against the malefaction of Eve.

The tempests and tumults, floods or famines, tycoons or tornados, epidemics or earthquakes are, likewise, the sufferance of nature. In the casual calamitous operations of nature, the nature seems to be aberrated, yet neither of such calamities has been, nor could ever be, traced to some disorder within itself. There is no evidence that these or even greater calamities could ever impair the intrinsic mechanism of nature so as to require any repair.

The blame has, therefore, to be fixed elsewhere.

The *Vedic* war between the divinities and devilities referred to in the *Aitereya Brahmin,* is a state of hostility between gods and demons, and is allegory for the good and the evil aspects in the human freedom of will.

The enlightened commentators on the **Vedas** are now agreed that the terms *Devas* and *Asuras,* standing for gods and demons, are employed as metaphor, which stand socially for the trash and bad characters, and psychologically for the pious and the perverted tendencies in man.

The malice in man maligns the nature. The misdemeanour of man is mischief to the nature. The perversion of man is pollution of nature, and environment is only glimpse of nature conceived in its five components of sky, air, fire, water and earth and the vast creaturehood produced by a combination of these elements.

A spoonful of wine may not inebriate its consumer but an inordinate and boozy doze is liable to make the body and brain upset and shaken. Casual and stray acts by deviation from duty, may not, likewise, offend the nature but **a spate of heinous crimes clamped on society, the massive terrorism gripping the world, and other known and unabated venalities and distractions, increasing voluptuousness and all varieties of alienation from spirituality, are liable to make the nature mourn and express its resentment in unpredictable forms.**

The global conferences and academic discourses and seminars, with their common agenda confined to toxic emissions and hazardous chemical discharges, though worried from global warming, puncturing of the ozone layer or deforestation and extinction of species, which too are causes contributed by man, have failed to allude to the above surrealities far more responsible for environmental disaster and imbalance in nature.

This proposition of topical urgency may hence be assayed with a pensive probe into the compass and expanse of the cosmic environment, in its analytic details.

CHAPTER 2

COSMIC ENVIRONMENT – COMPASS AND EXPANSE

SYNOPSIS

1. The Mystique of the Real and Unreal
2. Evolutionary Process
3. The Evolutes
4. Expanse of Cosmic Environment
5. Environment as One Cosmic Whole
6. Meaning of Environment

1. The Mystique of the Real and Unreal

What an awe it would have been if there were nothing, but the scriptures so assume that there was nothing (in the beginning).

The Genesis, called the *First Book of Moses,* says:

> "And the earth was without form and void; and darkness was upon the face of the deep......"

The *Rigvada*[1] declares that there was, then, neither the sky, nor the atoms, neither life, nor death, neither day nor night, and all was a deep abyss of fluid.

The *Manusmriti*[2] states:

> "Then this world was pitch dark indiscernible, that is, without distinguishing marks, unthinkable and incomprehensible, in a kind of deep sleep all over."

---

1. Thus/129.
2. 1/5.

The seventh canto of the *Taittiriya Upnishad* enunciates:

> "Hencebefore was the unreal, thence was born the real."

The gloss of *unreal* put upon the term *nothing* means that what prevailed heretobefore was not nothingness but was simply unreal. **Nothingness is logical impossibility, because *something* cannot come from *nothing*.**

Lord Krishna denies nothingness by construing the term 'real' and 'unreal' in relation to each other, as he affirms[1]:

> "The unreal has no existence, and the real never ceases to be; the reality of both has, thus, been conceived by the seers."

Nothingness is grammatically fallacious. In saying *it is not,* the *not* is in relation to the object of which the *it* is the subject, and the auxiliary verb *is* serves as predicative of the relation between the i*t* and the n*ot*. In saying *this is not,* the sayer, in all goodness, affirms primarily and fundamentally, the existence of 'this' "which is not" and the expression "which is not" implies "which is not (manifest)."

In saying **A** is not **B** the adverb *not* neither negates **A** nor nullifes **B** but is explicative of the difference what **A** does not have of **B** and what **B** lacks of. **A** is real but, at the same time, unreal in relation to **B**, and *vice versa.*

The *real* and the *unreal* are ideological terms, that is, terms of art. Understood in the metaphysical sense, the word *unreal* refers to the temporary and the transient; and the word *real* connotes the eternal and the imperishable.

---

1. The *Bhagwadgita,* 2/16.

The term *unreal* signifies the ever-changing physical body and the senses as well as their objects, including all that is material in this objective world. So when it is said that the *unreal* has no existence, the implication is that it was non-existent even before the time of its so called existence, and will be non-existent afterwards. Therefore, in reality, it does not exist even when it appears to exist.

The *real* connotes the supreme primordial reality, the spirit which is all pervading. The words "It never ceases to be" are intended to convey the idea that at no point of time and under no circumstance, the spirit undergoes any change or ceases to exist. The *real* renamed is the state of being, constant and unchangeable, whereas the *unreal* is in a state of becoming and change.

In the theistic religions, the *real* is denominated as the spirit of God, as the *Genesis* asserts: *And the spirit of God moved upon the face of the water,* even when *darkness was upon the face of the deep.* In the vedic pantheism, the *real* assumes the name of the *Ataman* as the *Aitereyopnishad*[1] proclaims:

The Ataman alone existed in the beginning and nothing else.

In order to dispel the confusion apparently gripping the words 'real' and 'unreal', the seers substituted these words respectively by the terms 'manifest' and 'unmanifest'. In the *Rigveda*[2] the word *'Apraket'* is synonym of the unmanifest. In the *Manusmriti*[3], the word 'Avyakta' is again the synonym of the unmanifest. The *Bhagwadgita*[4] states:

---

1. 1/1.
2. 10/129/2.
3. 1/6.
4. 2/28.

> "Before birth, beings are not manifest, at death they return to the unmanifest again. They are manifest only in the interim between birth and death".

The *Bhagwadgita*[1] reiterates the same thing by stating:

> "All embodied beings emanate from the unmanifest, at the onset of the cosmic day; and at the cosmic nightfall, they merge in the same unmanifest".

The *Bhagwadgita*[2] propounds the same thing, again, with a bit of difference in the expression:

> "During the final dissolution, all beings merge into the *prakriti* which is the primordial cause, and at the commencement of creation, they are issued forth again."

The unreal is, therefore, not non-being but is only unmanifest being. 'Unmanifest' and 'manifest' may be represented respectively by the more plebeian terms as the latent and the patent.

The patent effect is intervolved in its latent cause, maintains the Samkhya School of Indian Philosophy. The cause is latent and unmanifest; the effect becomes patent and manifest, just as the tree is latent and unmanifest in its seed; and the tree is the patent effect or the manifest form of the seed. The unreal or unmanifest is the cause, the source or the womb of the effect which became patent and manifest by its own instinctive pull.

The proposition was yet simplified in the *Mahabharata*[3] where even the terms 'manifest' and 'unmanifest', that is the *Vyakta* and *Avyakta*, were

---

1. 8/18.
2. 9/7.
3. *Stree Parva*, 2/13.

substituted by the terms *darshan* and *adarshan*, meaning respectively as the perceptible and the imperceptible, stating that the material world emanates from the imperceptible and recedes again in the imperceptible.

The imperceptible is the same thing as unmanifest, since it is only the manifest which is capable of being perceived through one or the other of the five sense organs, and that which cannot be perceive through the senses is simply unmanifest.

The Sun, the Moon, the starry firmament, the Earth, the rivers, mountains and all physical objects are manifest. The five elements, of sky, the fire, the air, the water and the earth and their respective attributes of sound, colour, touch, taste and smell, too, are manifest since these can be felt and perceived by all, through their senses. All that the universe is composed of, to the extent the capacity of the senses or the capacity of man to launch in the yonder space may permit, would all be perceptible and, therefore, manifest. Yet what is manifest in the creaturehood is their respective frame of body, and that which is still imperceptible is the spirit which pervades the entire frame. The universe, on the same analogy, is the outer frame forming the peripheries of the cosmos, and the cosmic spirit, which the *Genesis* names as the spirit of God, or what the *Upnished*[1] conceives as the *Atma*, which alone existed before the coming into being of the universe, is unmanifest and imperceptible. So, the proposition that the real comes from the *unreal*[2] has to be logically reversed that the objects which are perceptible would be unreal, because they are perishable and transient whereas the spirit which is eternal and immutable is alone real though imperceptible.

---

1. *Aitereyopnished,* 1/1.
2. *Taittiriyopnishad,* 2/7.

The material objects bereft of spirit and the animate beings, equipped both with spirituality and materiality, provide evidence that the monistic principle in unmanifest, manifested itself into a duality of the spirit and the matter, roughly, mind and matter, though the idea has attempted to describe the same into different modes of nomenclatures and, thereby to deploy itself into different theories, though not difficult for each to reconcile with the other. The physical sciences generally refer to this duality as the energy and the matter. The Samkhya School of philosophy denominates them as the *Purusha* and the *prakriti*. The Vedanta school alludes to them as the *Brahman* and the *Maya*. The *Upanishad*[1] names the two as the *pran* and the *rayi*. From point of view of creation, the two are named respectively as the *Deva*, that is a deity, which is not subject to the cycle of births and deaths, and the *Bhoota*, which is subject to the process of births and deaths. With reference to the activity of the *Yajna*, understood by all as the process of offering oblations into the sacred fire, the two denote, again, the *agni* which is the consumer, and the *soma*, that which is consume by fire; and no religion the world over has been without the conception of two opposite or polar principles.

All these theorizations bring to bear that the primordial principle known as the unmanifest is neither spirit alone nor matter alone, but potentially both spirit and matter intervolved and indistinct when unmanifest but, when diffused, become distinct functionaries or principalities when manifest, and the perceptible legerdemain is an interaction, an interplay or the interfusion of the two.

The answer to the inquisition why after all the unmanifest should manifest itself is palpably simple

1. *Prashnopnishad.*

without any sophistication. The unmanifest manifests itself because of its own indomitable desire, because it cannot help the upsurge of its libido. There is an instinctive pull to unleash its potency or to release its incubated energy. The *Rigveda*[1] employs, for this desire, the term *Kama* which denotes the erotic principle, epitomized as the *manaso retah,* that is the seed of the mind, to be better conceived as the *nous* coiled unto the unmanifest. In the *Upanishads,* this impulse has been defined in various terms having no etymological variance. He desired (*so Kamyat*) says the *Taittiriyopnishad.*[2] The *Aitereyopnishad*[3] says "he cogitated (*sa Eekshat*). The *Taittiriyopnishad*[4] reiterates "He suffered penances" (*sa tapotapyat*), a process simply denoting an incubative or the gestative state, a state of concentration and conservation of energy prior to its liberation. In the *Bible (Genesis),* this onset of desire is expressed in plainest terms as *Let there be*. "Let there be" is the decree of the desire. With an immense input of the desire, the unmanifest became two-dimensional in its manifestation. The *Upnishad*[5] has described this state as a state of fear, the phobia of isolation or loneliness, and answers why the monistic principle became dualistic. Since it is impossible for one alone to dally, and the one alone cannot indulge into his own self, therefore, He became two in order to enjoy, yet retaining its compactness as one, just as the two halves studded together in a corn of cereal.

Manifestation is just sport for the unmanifest, and deployment of itself into creation is recreation of the unmanifest. The function of creation is revelation of the

1. 10/129/4.
2. 2/6.
3. 1/1/3; 1/3/1.
4. 2/6.
5. *Brihadaranyak,* 1/4.

unmanifest. The function of creation, if can, thus, be assigned to the exercise of dualisation of the unmanifest into two interdependent entities of spirit and matter. The process onward is only an evolutionary process.

2. Evolutionary Process

The unmanifest, in its indistinct alloy of the real and the unreal, designated in the *Vishnu Purana*[1] as the main and subtle or the salient primeval cause in its deep, dark, abysmal nescience, recoiled unto itself in equilibrium, becomes turbulent and agitated by the onset of the desire to become manifest, and the first step towards its manifestation, devised by itself, is its dualisation into the basal matter and the spirit, denominated respectively as the *Pradhan* and the *Purusha*. The term *Pradhan* denotes the basal matter, that is, the material base of the universe whereas the term *Purusha* stands for sentience or consciousness. In his commentary on the *Bhagwadgita*,[2] Shankaracharya has defined the term Purusha as the ubiquitous all pervading principle. The first, that is, the *Pradhan*, accepted in the *Samkhya* School of Indian Philosophy, is the *Prakriti*, that is the nature at large, or the primordial matter, which is inert but ever dynamic whereas the *Purusha* which is a stable, immutable conscious principle, is endowed with the cognitive, conative and emotive faculties and never suffers change, except the modifications in its consciousness. The onward cosmocraft is the interplay and interaction of these two principles, complimentary to each other.

The first byproduct of the interplay of these two principles is the *Mahat* which represents the intellect.

It may not be difficult to comprehend that the process of dualisation of the unmanifest into the material and the

---

1. 1/2.
2. 8/4.

spiritual bases, should naturally have caused the explosion of the deep abyss of darkness which was the primal content of the unmanifest, an activity similar to the Big Bang, or, may be, several bangs, minor or major, recognised by modern science.

In the Indian thought, this activity is compared with the activity of the eruption of the cosmic egg, the *Brahmanda,* with a compound of two words, *Brahma,* and the *anda,* which denotes the progenitor or the father of entire creaturehood, represented as the cosmic egg.

The *Manusmriti*[1] delineates this in a terse statement that after residing in that egg for a full year, which is not the mundane year but the period of an eternity till the time of fresh creation after the last deluge, the period during which the creation sustains, known as the cosmic day, and the period till the state of dissolution lasts, denoting the cosmic night or the sleep of the *Lord,* called in the *Durga saptashati*[2] as the *Yoganidra,* or the annihilative sleep, the *Lord* of his own, split the egg into two by brooding on His own body and from these two halves, He formed the sky and the earth, and between them the mid-space, the eight-fold dimensions and the eternal place of the waters.

The *Holy Bible*[3] describes it, in the same vein:

> "And God said let there be light, and there was light, that it was good; and God divided the light from the darkness.
>
> "And God called the light day and the darkness he called night. And the evening and the morning were the first day.

---

1. 1/12-13.
2. Ch. I
3. *Genesis.*

> "And God said let there be firmament in the midst of the waters and let it divide the waters from the waters."

Whether the bang or bangs or the eruption of the egg, both are in the nature of a blast or explosion and what is relevant is the cause and the consequence thereof.

The conserved heat going above its apogee is liable to an outburst. For instance, when milk is heated in a pot, the heat generated in the substance starts fizzling in the first instance and when reaching its climax, it starts boiling out. The egg too, would erupt when the inner incubation reaches its culmination. The condensed heat gets into a concussion and, finally, gushes out by its inner vibrating force; and brings about some simultaneous and synchronized consequences.

The explosion, blast or eruption, whatever be the appropriate term for this activity, creates a space, and this consequence is automatic in proportion to the quantum of its vibration. The accumulated heat becomes a massive lump of fire and is projected out in the space caused by the explosion.

The space so created becomes the firmament denominated in the Vedic schools of philosophy as the *aakash*, and the massive fiery ball stays in the space as the *Sun*.

Creation of the space or the *aakash* and the placement of the Sun in the *aakash* is a double implication of the very first event of the unmanifest becoming manifest. In the *Rigveda*[1] this first born celestial entity is demonstrated as the *Hiranyagarbha*, literally meaning the "golden nucleus", deified as the Lord of all beings and the bearer and the ordainer of the whole universe. The description comes in the form of a question as to which

1. 10/121.

of the deities man is supposed to make his offerings for; and the answer was that all offerings are to be made to this *Hiranyagarbha,* which is the first and the foremost, and chieftain, of the celestial bodies.

The ideation or the formation of other planets is yet simpler. The explosion of a cracker or other petard reveals that apart from its central blast, numbers of sparks are emitted around, because of the vibrative force releasing thorough its blasts. When the Sun emerged out of the explosion of the deep abyss of darkness, lumps of fiery matter must have flied off the main fiery globe, and settled through the natural cooling process, as different planets, and their satellites. Theorization of the same, may, otherwise, be ascribed to the attrition of the atoms, entering in the composition of the firmament itself.

The ether, the firmament, the sky, or the heavens are, in fact, no exact synonym of the *Samskrit* word, *the aakash* which, in the Vedic metaphysics, is not a void or blank emptied space, but is a substance, basal substance, holding all matter and material phenomena. The other elements, namely, air, fire, water and earth, are gradual and consecutive modification or catalysis of the *aakash* itself. The atomic stuff being electro-magnetically charged, and the atoms, of their own, are attracted to or detracted from each other. In their process of constant attrition, they can stick together to form a mass, or a smaller or bigger lump, and though the process might take epochnating eras, the stars, planets and galaxies are, or can be, formed this way alone.

The dualisation of the unmanifest, into matter or energy, the *Prakriti* and the *Purusha* of the *Samkhya* School of philosophy, is only palpable principle. Since the unmanifest is both spirit and matter, the manifest cannot be different but is a blend of both.

The cosmos is neither matter alone, nor spirit alone but is both spirit and matter all around. The spirit and the material frame of the animate creatures is both, as an endowment of the cosmic alchemy.

The first evolute being the Sun, and the first evolute, according to *Samkhya* metaphysics, being the *Mahat, Buddhi* or the intellect, the Sun stands as the cosmic intellect, and henceforth can be traced the other evolutes.

3. The Evolutes

Evolution is a term of wide import, so as to denote every change, inclusive both of development and decay. Evolution is a process of flux and dynamicity, whether upward or downward. A crude but common phenomenon of human life may bring home the point. Right from the embryonic stage till the declining age, the human frame is in a developing state till youth and then starts decaying with the onset of old age; and from initial childhood till completion of his centenary, he is the same self yet every moment under change. What suffers change is the physical frame and what defies change is the spirit pervading the physical frame. **The body is phenomenal; the spirit is noumenal.**

The phenomenal is fleeting, changing, dynamic and inconsient. The noumenal is immutable, impeccable, impalpable, omnificent and conscient.

From the deep abyss of darkness, when there was nothing, which Aurbindo[1] describe as the "time before the gods awake", when the unmanifest was all aplomb in itself, the environs of the cosmos evolve in manner beyond comprehension, after the last deluge, through the buoyance of the full recharge of its energy by dynamitising afresh to spring into action the event of dualisation of itself by becoming two out of one.

1. Savitri, Canto 1, line 1.

This dualisation, at the initial stage of manifestation, is notional bifurcation into two separate entities as the *Manusmriti*[1] says:

> "After residing in the egg for a full year, that Lord on his own, split the egg in two by brooding on his own body. From these two halves, He formed the sky and the earth, and between them the mid-space, the eight directions and the eternal place of the waters."

The deep abyss of the pervading darkness, which is the egg, or the embryonic stage of the unmanifest, is the cosmic night, and the event of its bifurcation into the firmament and the Sun, represents the dawn of the cosmic day. The *Manusmriti*[2] has given a concise account of the duration of this day and night, and the ages comprising this day have been given, in a proper sequence, naming the first age as the *Krit,* followed by the subsequent ages of *Treta, Dwapara* and *Kali,* though not specifically named in the *Manusmriti* but so named in the *Puranas* compiled by the sage *Vedvyas.* The *Krit* age, according to the *Manusmriti,* is said to last 4000 years. It is preceded by a twilight lasting 400 years and followed by a twilight of the same length. For each of the three subsequent ages, as also for the twilights that precede and follow them, the first number of the thousands and the hundreds is progressively diminished by one. These four ages computed at the very beginning as lasting 12000 years, are said to constitute a single day of the gods, which means the age of the celestial bodies in the integrated whole of one solar system. The sum total of such 1000 celestial ages should be counted as a single cosmic day, with the cosmic night having the very same duration.

---

1. 1/12,13.
2. 1/68-73.

It is obvious that so long as the unmanifest rests in its deep abyssal slumber, described in the *Markandeya Purana*[1] as the *Yoganidra,* or the ascetic sleep, there was no concept of time. The time begins to run from movement of the planets around the Sun after its onset.

The Sun being the soul of the universe is in a constant state of throbbing. The throb of the heart in the human body is derived only from the throb of the Sun, since the human frame is conceived as the cosmos in miniature, and the throb of the heart denotes a moment, equivalent roughly to a bit more than the human concept of a second. The rotation of each planet round the Sun in their respective orbits, represents the year respectively of each planets, varying in accordance with its own velocity. The computation of the ages in the *Manusmriti* is from point of view of the rotation of the earth around the Sun.

The bifurcation of one into two is the cosmic idea to come into creativeness. The notional idea of bifurcation of the unmanifest into *Prakriti* and *Purusha,* matter and spirit, practically becomes the condition precedent to procreation of the species. The function ideationally is a conjugal function as much as the blending of the spirit and matter for purpose of creation as the union of a male and a female[2] for purpose of procreation which is a crude activity for the subtle function of nature.

The notional bifurcation of the unmanifest into the two principles of matter and spirit became manifest in the establishment of the firmament and the Sun, representing the respective material and the spiritual sides of the unmanifest, neither of them being matter alone or spirit alone, but one predominantly matter and

1. *Durga Saptashati,* Chapter 1.
2. See *Brihadaranyak Upnishad,* 1/4/3.

the other predominantly spirit, and the predominance is throughout preserved in the fundamental cosmogenic variance between the male and the female counterparts in their prognostic function. The firmament is not without its spiritual content but is predominantly the finest of the matter, as the source of any material embodiment. The Sun is, likewise, not without its share of atomic matter but is predominantly the source of all life, energy and consciousness in the world.

In the firmament, spirituality is latent but materiality, patent. In the Sun, spirituality is patent but materiality, latent, though both emanate from one and the same principle which is the womb of matter and spirit both. The process is release of the matter from the spirit and simultaneously, a release of the spirit from the matter.

The assertion that the Sun is the only source of light, life, energy, consciousness and intelligence, has positive evidence as well as ethical conviction.

The positive evidence is two-fold – the astronomical and the bio-causal.

The Sun alone is the universe in an efficient conscious way, by keeping planets within their orbits yet always tending to the Sun and this activity with no possibility of deviation, is itself evidence both of efficiency and consciousness.

The penetration of the rays into the air, oceans and earth is scientific explanation of avian, aquatic and terrestrial life. The origin of life is traced to the alchemy of lighter compounds diffused freely in nature, in the substantive forms of carbon, hydrogen, oxygen and nitrogen, combining with each other resulting in the basic compounds of water, ammonia and methane. The transcombination of these simple compounds resulted into the formation of more sophisticated compounds like glucose, glycerine and the fatty acids, and the process continues until the creation of the virus considered to be the first representative of embodied life.

Composed only of nucleic acid, the virus reacted upon another compound of protein, and a combination of the two had brought about the origin of the nucleo-protein endowed with the faculty of reproduction. The first step towards evaluation of animate existence was the origin of the appetitive life, capable of nothing other than being possessed with the appetite of reproduction.

The fermentation had to soon discover that even the crude appetence could not be prolonged without ingestion of energy. The primal life arrested in the chrysalis of a single cell aspired to come into contact with a source of energy. The Sun being the single source of energy, the cellular life came into communion with the Sun. The Sun is the nucleus of the universe, and since a communion could be possible from nucleus to nucleus, the cellular life, so far without a nucleus, had to develop a nucleus for the generation, into it of a substance known as the chlorophyll, meant as an absorbent of solar energy with the advantage of the appetitive life evolving into the vegetative life. The Sun as the centre of the universe, became also the sustainer of life. This proves the sustenance of life as a singular, continuous, uniform phenomenon making it possible for the components of creation to share life on unlike but gradually ascending order. In the ascending order of creation, the vegetative life evolved into the animal life or the instinctive life which had finally culminated into the meditative life of the homosapien.

The ethical aspect, yet simpler, is the integrality of the principles of light, life, consciousness and intelligence, which are more or less developed gradually from cruder to the complex states of life, evolved from its simple to sophisticated forms of consciousness and intelligence in the emergence of life. **All consciousness is consciousness of being alive**. Higher intelligence leads to higher attainments; and the species differ from each other in proportion to the degree of intelligence endowed on them. Intelligence is manifestation or modification of the power to think and to will, in an ordered hierarchy of one and the same stream of life.

The following may, thus, be taken as some of the **fundamental propositions** in the process of cosmogenesis:

(i) The dualisation of the unmanifest in its manifestation is an indistinct alloy of the spirit and the matter, and the bisection in view of the operation of the two principles is not actual dissection. Both operate in an inseparable blend. The spirit is born of the matter; and the matter born of the spirit.

(ii) There is no cosmic space or element bereft of the spirit. The spirit of the *Purusha* is ubiquitous and omnipresent. The *Yajurveda*[1] says that the *Purusha* is everywhere, be it any time in the past or in the future. It is God which is all-pervasive in each particle of it, states the *Ishavasyopnishad*[2] though the spirit in the universe is diffused whereas that in the animate being, it is concentrated.

(iii) The mighty Sun enters into the life of all mortals[3]

(iv) The Sun is the first cosmic evolute, emerging out of the blend of spirit and matter and stays as the source and sustainer of all life.

---

1. 31/1/2.
2. First *Hymn*.
3. *Rigveda*, 5/58/3.

(v) The Sun as the first evolute, survives as the cosmic intellect, and the human intellect, the more or less in animate being, is only Sun incarnate.

The next evolute in sequence after the *Mahat* or intellect was the *Ahankar* representing the ego, as has been unanimously held by the *Puranas*[1] and the *Samkhya school* of Indian philosophy. The word *ahankar* may literally stand for egoism but metaphysically it simply denotes 'I-ness'. The intellect is faculty of knowledge; and the first thing the self knows is its own existence. "I am" is the first incidence of knowledge. All other things, whenever and wherever known, are part of knowledge of self, by the self and for the self.

"I think, therefore, I am", to the French philosopher Rene Descartes, was so solid and so certain that all the most extravagant suppositions of the sceptics were incapable of upsetting it. "No demon" howsoever cunning could deceive Descartes if he did not exist. While the thinker wanted to think every thing as false, it must necessarily be that the thinker exists. *Cogito ergo sum* is known as Descartes's *cogito* and the process by which it is reached is called *Cartesian Doubt.*

In the very beginning it was the *Atma,* that is the self and the first thought that occurred to the self was that there was nothing else than 'I'; and therefore, as the *Brihadaranyak Upnished*[2] says, the *Atma* or the self uttered *"aham"*.

The *Samskrit* term for 'I' is *Aham;* and there is striking and curious phonetic similarity between the *Samskrit* term *Aham* and the English expression "I am". Even the name given to the person on birth, by his parents is

1. See *Vishnu Purana,* 1/2/33.
2. 1/4/1.

secondary, since in identifying himself with the name *X*, *Y* or *Z*, the one so named utters in the first instance "I am" and thereafter speaks of his name *X*, *Y* or *Z*, and this 'I am' is always the prefix to the name borne by the person.

These two psychic evolutes were then followed by the material elements. The element of *Aakash* or the firmament, as the prime natural element, being the bearer of the Sun, the Moon, the galaxies and thousands of stars, is accepted as the cause of other natural elements but, in itself, the first evolute of the manifest cosmos. When the cosmic egg erupted or the deep nescient abyss exploded, the Sun and the firmament must have emerged together and simultaneously, yet as the container of all the cosmic constituents, it is counted as the first. The egg when erupts creates its own space on account of the vital push of its incubated vibration. The first outburst of the abyss of darkness, likewise from the gush of its vibration, ripped apart to create a space out of itself, and the *Aakash* is only the space so created automatically in that process of ripping apart. The inner incubated vibration because of its own emissive force filled the firmament all around and the gaseous substance of air, thus, became the element counted as second and in succession to the *aakash.* The air condensed in its turn, and smouldered by the heat of the space energy, became fire. The fire yet condensed and in its contact with the frigid or gelid parts of space turned into water. By the combined interaction of heat and air both, the water, gradually, became foamed and, fuzzy and, later, by the same combined alchemy, became mud and thereafter dough and eventually dried up into crusts and layers and through the passage of epochs, the earth assumed its own form of land. The earth, produced the flora, and the cereal, as produced from the vegetative content of the earth, generated the animate creaturehood, and the cereal they consumed enabled them to inseminate and thereby multiply their own race.

The course of further evolution as traced in the *Samkhya* school of Indian philosophy delineates, the air or the *Vayu*, the fire or the *Agni*, the water or the *Jal*, and the earth or the *Prithvi*, each endowed with their intrinsic, inalienable attributes, named as *Tanmatras* or the *subtle senses* respectively of the sound, touch, sight, taste and smell, then giving rise to these five senses. In an animate creature, particularly in the man at the apex, these senses became posited in the emergence of the corresponding sense accessories of the ear, skin, eyes, tongue and nose, capable to feel and experience these sensations and, then, finally, the process culminated in the development of the five motor organs of the physical frame, namely, the mouth, the belly, the anus, the hands and the feet, meant to activise the body to function in an orderly course. The numbers of these evolutes, thus, stand, in all, to twenty-four. The *Purusha* or the spirit, the *Prakriti* or the matter, the *Mahat* or the intellect, the *Ahankar* or the ego, which is I-nees, the five elements or the manifest substances of the *Aakash* or the firmament, the air, the fire, the water and the earth, along with their five subtle senses of the sound or the *shabda*, the touch or the *sparsh*, the *rupa* or the light or the chromatic sense, and the *rasa* or the taste and *gandha* or the *smell*; and these fourteen coupled with their outfits of the abovesaid five sense organs and the five motor organs, thus, make up the total of twenty-four evolutes.

What is notable is that the physical and the psychological evolution both go together and the process of evolution is a psycho-physical parallelism.

What can curiously be denoted as nature at large is the combine, in whatever state, of the above five elements of the *aakash, vayu, agni, jala* and *prithvi.* **This nature at large is the cosmic environment which is an integrated absolute whole not liable to be viewed in fragments.** The expanse of the cosmic environment though boundless, has yet been accounted for in the imagery of seers.

4. Expanse of Cosmic Environment

In the imagery of seers, the limitless expanse of the cosmic environment, has broadly been conceived to consist of seven zones, better called orbs, which do not denote any precise celestial boundary but have been conceivably devised on basis of the allotropy of one or the other of these five vital elements, in their recurringally preceding but latent states.

A vivid description of the compass of these cosmic orbs is available in the *Purana* literature and a reference can, for sake of convenience, be made only to the *Vishnu Purana.*[1] The orbs, conceived in their elliptical compass, the cosmos as a whole would geometrically comprise of 360°, on the assumption of a circular phenomenon, and these degrees are just an apprehended imagery in the same way as latitudes and longitudes of the earth have been comprehended in theory though accurately portrayed in the atlas.

The seers in the conjecture of their measurement have used the standard of a *Yojan,* which is equal to eight miles or 14000yards, approximating to 12.8 kms. Thus, the nomenclature of the orbs is esoteric and the distance from one to the other only imaginary, since no mortal being has ever been able to correctly measure and precisely state the expanse of cosmic space, in any standard measurement, though the prevailing faith

1. 2/7.

always ascribes a mathematical accuracy to the intuition of seers.

The allotropy of the named orbs, rolled one over the other, in a serried sequence, represents a specific form or pattern of life. **Each orb has a distinct life content, and it follows that life evolves not on or in the earth but in the named celestial orbs.** The earth only nurtures, generates, produces or reproduces the life as formulated by the celestial alchemy, and plays the maternal role in furbishing the given life pattern with its physical frame, and is, hence, revered as the mother earth.

The region upto which the light of Sun and the Moon can traverse is known, with its seas, rivers and mountains, as the Earth. Equal to the expanse and the circumspection of the Earth, is the expanses and circumspection of the celestial firmament that is, the horizon, popularly represented as the biosphere. The solar orb is distant from the earth by one lakh *yojan*, equivalent roughly to the metric distance of 12, 80,000 kms. From the solar mass, the lunar orb is stated to stand at the same distance as is the solar orb from the earth; and from the lunar orb, it covers the same distance upto the yonder starry vault.[1]

Two lakh *yojan* above the starry vault is the location of the planet Mercury; and, again, the same distance lies in between Mercury and Venus, and equally at the same distance from Venus is the location of the Mars. Traversing further, the same distance from Mars stands the planet Jupiter. The same distance falls between Jupiter and Saturn.

From Saturn up to the constellation of the seven stars, exists the *Ursa Major*, also know as the Great Bear. Spread between the earth and the Ursa Major, the entire

1. *Vishnu Purana*, 2/7.

spatial region is the firmament or the celestial space, classically conceived as the pantheon.

The seers having no mechanism except their vision in conjecturing these immeasurable distances, their coincidence or compatibility or incompatibility with the calculation of the modern astronomy is hardly relevant when the enormity of the distance and the identity of the named celestial bodies are not in dispute.

It is common knowledge that the creaturehood in flesh and blood is denied to the pantheon. The spirit or the content of part of the pantheon above the biosphere, can only be psychic, mentational or astral, known in the Hindu Genetics of rebirth as the *linga sharir,* or the subtle body which traverses after death to the heavens, enveloping in itself yet another finer stuff known as the *Karana Sharir,* or the causal body, responsible for rebirth.

The causal bodies have their individuality retained in themselves for purpose of rebirth, once taken apart from masses of the various causal parameters out of which these individual causal bodies are constituted and, then, thrown into the cycle of births and rebirths of real species. This phenomenon explains the generation of organic bodies on earth.

A hundred thousands *yojan* above Ursa Major is the region of the Pole Star, forming the nucleus of the entire Orion of the spatial tract comprising earth, the pantheon and the Great Bear, forming one trinary or the *Trilok,* as conceived in the scriptures.

This triality accommodates the entire starry vault, harbouring all the planets and the galaxies formed by the interaction of stardust. Tiny grains of stardust, first collide and then stick together, conglomerate and conglutinate due to their electrical attraction coupled with attrition and, thus, go on forming lumps; and this explains the genesis of the planets, the stars and galaxies in a uniform but unending cosmological process.

This affirms the credibility of an ever expanding universe. The orbicular configuration of the earth and all other planets and stars is itself evidence of the cosmos being itself orbicular. It is because of the orbicular pressure of the space energy which orbiculates the mass of the planets and stars. The orbicularity, or any circumferential phenomenon, must inevitably refer to a center. Circumference without a centre is a geometrical impossibility. **Circumference is only multidimensional movement, or extension of the centre itself. All radii are liable to tend to one concentric point. The centre is nothing but a point and the radii are diffusive extensions of the point.** The orbital expanses of the universe is spontaneous effect of the outburst of the concentrated energy of the centre, and once the conserved momentum of the centre is let loose, and there being no hindering obstacle, the expanse of the centre is bound to be incessantly ellipsoid extending into an ever-expanding space. The Hindu scriptures, therefore, testify the existence of thousands, millions and billions of universes uniform in their process though varied in their content in accordance with the difference in the ambulation of the pulls and pressures of the space energy on different tracts of space at different points of time.

Consuming a duration of one crore years from the aforesaid triality, covering the region from the earth below up to the *Ursa Major* above, being a constellation of the Seven Stars with its *Samskrit* synonym as the *Sapt Rishis,* is the vast ethereal space, conceived in the scriptures as the *Maharlok,* which is the abode of the subtle emancipated souls subsisting till end of the cosmic cycle, and denominated in the scriptures as the *Rishis.* **The entities denominated as the *Rishis* have the prime**

role in the origin of life on earth. At a distance of two crore *Yojan* from the region called the *Maharlok,* is the stretch of yet another astral region, as the *Janalok,* which is the habitat of the purest spirits, conceived in the scriptures as issued forth from the cosmic creator, named as *Brahma.* Covering a space upto eight crore *Yojan* from this *Janalok* is the austereal region, known as the *Tapalok* occupied by the austere divinities representing the divine cosmic causalities which are immune from effect of fire. They are not subject to immolation, which connotes the absence of the element of fire in that region. Finally, at a distance of twelve crore *yojan* from this *Tapalok* is the primeval auric region, defined as the *Satyaloka* also called the *Brahmaloka* where dwell the unborn immortals, immune from the cycle of births, deaths and rebirths.

These distances being glimpses of the esoteric imagery of the visionaries, may be taken not as total illusion but rightly as an accurate allusion to the boundless and ever-abounding universe, virtually, connoting not the extremity of the universe but verily as the limit of the imagery of the seers. **There are no conceivable termini of the cosmic compass.** The distances conceived in crores are simple euphemism for endlessness.

The composition of the whole cosmos has, thus, been conceived as the sum total of three trinalities, as under;

(i) The earth with the solar and lunar orbs up to the polestar;

(ii) The sphere of the polestar with the *Maharlok* upto the *Janalok;*

(iii) The *Janalok* with the *Tapalok* upto the *Satyaloka.*

The denizens of these regions, in a serried sequence above the earth, are not persons or personalities but are only potentialities, not products but only principles; not carnalities but only causalities.

They are not living entities but life-giving alchemies, the higher one being superior and subtler than its each corresponding lower. Life descends from them down to the earth in sequent orders, modifying and metamorphosing itself in consonance with its own cosmic accoutrement.

The source and stuff of life being one systematic whole, it is not possible to segregate or alienate it into different bounded segments. **The environment is biologically, chemically and metaphysically, one integrated cosmic whole.**

5. Environment as One Cosmic Whole

The vision of seers in viewing the cosmos in several orbicularities is not conceptual convenience but is based on veridical analysis of the allotropy peculiar to each orbicular phase of the cosmos with no dividing line or vaulted boundaries; and it would be sacrilegious to view one or the other orbicular tract in isolation. The one immutable principle and the one universal system, prevails and pervades alike from the largest planet down to the smallest particle. This and that, or here and there, is constituent part of the same macrocosmic whole governed by the same cosmic law, and any fragmentary view is a human foible.

The delimitation of the environment upto the earth and its biosphere alone, is to disdain the entire cosmic allotropy and alchemy. A drop of poison at any point on the surface is liable to pollute the entire ocean, though it may be conceded that the fathomic volume of the sea is strong enough to quell the adverse effect of the little quantity of the venom let loose therein, in the same way as death of one single cell in a stout body may not suffice to damage the edifice of the body as a whole, yet the loss of a single cell is, to an extent, impairment of the mass of the organism. A thorn in the heel, a cut in the finger, a boil on the arm or a pain in the tooth, howsoever trivial, is panic to the self and a concern of the whole body.

Smoking a cigar in the auditorium, howsoever insignificant to the auditorium as a whole is all the same an injury to all the inmates of the auditorium compelled to be passive smokers. A fragmentary view of a given part of the whole is illogic since the source of life is not from down upward but from above downward as the *Kathopnishad*[1] and the *Bhagwadgita*[2] proclaim that the world is a tree with its roots above and its branches down.

Life on earth comes from above as continuous flow of animation right from the highest cosmic sphere down to the earth. Just as the global habitat cannot be viewed in isolation of the world as a whole including its oceans, mountains and forests, the globe itself cannot be viewed in isolation from the cosmos as a whole. **An event in the cosmos may have devastating effect on the globe and a havoc on the globe may become a cosmic hazard, since both are incidents of a given whole.**

The environment taken as a cosmic concept may now legitimately lead to the quest for a comprehensive meaning of the term 'environment'.

6. Meaning of Environment

The word 'environment' is grammatically the noun derived from the word 'environ' which, in the parts of speech, is a transitive verb. In the Random House Dictionary of the English Language, the word 'environ' is stated to mean:

> "to form a circle or ring round; surround, envelope."

1. 2/3.
2. 15/1.

The word 'environment' is then defined as follows:

> "1. the aggregate or surrounding things, condition or influences; 2. the act of environing; 3. the state of being environed; 4. something that environs."

The legal definitions of the word 'environment' do not precisely correspond with the literal or the philosophical meaning of this term. For example, the legal definition given in an Indian statute[1] states that:

> "'Environment' includes water, air and land and the interrelationship which exists among and between water, air and land, and human beings, other living creatures, plants, micro-organism and property."

The above definition has not defined the term 'land', and may be, the definition of that term, though relevant, was not necessary since 'land' is known to everybody as the part of the surface of earth above the water of oceans.

The definition under reference has included within its scope the water, again, left undefined, and there is implicit difficulty in defining 'water'. The land may have the same meaning here on earth or on any planet, because it denotes the surface, and the difference in its material composition, whether here or on any other planet, has no significance, because the crusty layers of soil, with all the possible differences in their agrarian quality, is common to all the planets, but the definition of water may involve a complexity.

The *Upnishad*[2] refers to four grades of water, substantially different from one another. The water in the regions above the polestar, that is, in the regions, namely the *Mah,* the *Janah,* the *Tapah* and the *Satya* regions, as

1. The Environment Protection Act, 1986, section 2(a).
2. *Aitereyopnishad,* 1/1/2.

have been described above, is denominated as the *ambh,* which, of course, is not potable water, but water in its fluid gaseous state. Below these, is the region comprising the polestar, the Sun the Moon and the starry vault, and water there is given the nomenclature of *marichi,* which again is not potable water but, in its quality and content, is different from that named as the *Ambh.* The word *marichi* denotes lustrous rays, and since the Sun and the Moon and other stars are sources of these rays, the water in this region has been conceived as synonymous with *marichi.* The water available on the surface of the earth, in rivers, lakes, wells, etc., has been named as the *mar.* The word *mar* refers to mortality and since the earth is the region of the mortals, the water on earth is justifiably given the name of *mar.* The fourth grade of water existing below the surface and in the bosom of the earth, is named as *aap.* These four grades are only different metamorphic states of one and the same substance assuming different forms in accordance with the allotropy of the different cosmic regions. The water in the river *Ganga* is known for its efficacious purity, because it is that mass of *ambh,* the first grade water, which getting heavier in its condensed form, descends down to the pedestal of the Sun and pushed by its rays to finally fall on the Himalaya, and the Ganga comes on earth from an orifice of the Himalayas.

The water in its primordial state stays as *ambh* in the regions beyond the polestar, and thence descends down to the solar region to become *marichi* and thence pouring down through the rains, it becomes *mar;* and, finally the water saturating in the crusts of earth beneath its surface, whether from the oceans or from crusts of the earth, becomes *aap,* but, viewed in its basic ingredients, it is one and the same substance althrough. The water as substance and as one of the cosmic constituents gradually differentiates itself in form in the order of its descent from the heavens down to the earth.

The cosmic fire, in the same way, has been classified into three. The *Rigveda,* in its very first hymn, deals with it as the *agni* of the earth, also known as the *pawak.* The very first hymn of the *Samaveda* deals with it as the fire comprising the solar mass, described in the scriptures as the *pawamana.* The *Yajurveda* has dealt with it in relation to the space energy as a whole, denominated as the *Shuchi;* and all these three are metamorphic states only of one cosmic substance, retaining its basic ingredients althrough. The *aakash* though described as consisting of various orbs or spheres, is one cosmic space without any formal partition. The land, too, is one and the same, and the difference from planet to planet is only physiographic. The fire, before or after its ignition is a reservoir of gaseous mass. The air, too, is a gaseous substance. The cosmic evolutes of *aakash,* air, fire, water and earth are constituents of nature as one and a whole, and interact with each other by device of one single cosmic spirit, and their systematic interaction is itself evidence of the spirituality of the cosmic environment as one and a whole, and all life comes from this environment.

CHAPTER 3

LIFE FROM ENVIRONMENT

SYNOPSIS

1. The Androgynous

Be it known as essence, attribute or nature, spirituality consists in the subjectivity of the spirit. Existence of spirit if proved, there is no further warrant for evidence of spirituality. Realization of the spirit is the man's ideal which has deployed itself into numerous philosophies, each different to reconcile with the other. The *Upanishads* recognise it as the *Atman.* The philosophies supple with religiosity, denominate it as the soul. In the philosophy of Plotinus it is the *nous.* In the *Gospel* of Saint John, it is the *logos.* In psychology, it is conceived as the *self* which is the most convenient euphemism for all these epithets. There is no dispute, however, that it is an entity and an end in itself, different from the physical frame. In the *Bhagwadgita*[1], this self is

1. 3/42, 43.

delineated as He, a pronoun in the third person; and the statement that precedes this He, is that the senses are said to be greater than the body; but greater than the senses is the mind; greater still than the mind, is the intellect and what is yet greater than the intellect is He, the Self. A distinction has been posed between the mind and the intellect, because the mind or the *Mana* is the enjoyer and employer of the senses, whereas the intellect, that is the *Buddhi*, dominates even the mind.

The *Kathopnishad*[1] metaphorically speaks of the body as a coach, and the senses as horses. Horses are possessed of life and are superior to the coach and can draw the chariot after them according to their will. Even so, the senses alone can take the body wherever they like; therefore, they are superior to or greater than the body, and are sensitive too. The body is perceptible whereas the senses are the perceivers and, hence, subtler than the body.

All said above, is simple philosophy. The otherness of the spirit than the body and the senses, is so certain and simple and the truth thereof so evident that it needs no other proof. After death, the body becomes entirely defunct and can neither move nor feel. There is, hence, something other than the body in functional animation, and that something departs from the body on death; and that something is spirit called by whatever name in whatever context. There is always the charioteer other than the chariot which enacts the whole show. The body is the vehicle for its activities and the senses are the apparatus through which it perceives, feels and witnesses events and accumulates experience and reciprocates with anything other than itself. It is through the body that the spirit acts and it is through the senses that it knows and

1. 1/3/3, 4.

what it knows is always the other than itself. **It is the craving for knowledge of the other which is both cause and purpose of creation.**

This duality of the knower and the known, and the process of knowing the other to the fullest, is the indomitable desire of the cognitive agent, known in the *Rigveda*[1] as the *Kama* and this cognitive agent is known as the person, designated in the *Vedas*[2] as the *Purusha;* and that of which the cognitive agent becomes cognisant, is the dynamic principle, the counterpart of the spirit, known as the *Prakriti* or the materiality at large. There being none other in the beginning, the cosmic cell had to split into two; one the knower, and other, the known. At a point of time antecedent to creation, the two are in a state of involution but from the point of the onset of creation, they get into a state of intervolution, and the process onward is handled by the two together acting in concert.

The repeated compossibility or the communion of the spirit and matter, finally succeeded in producing on earth an epicenic organism which, by its inner conative force, bifurcated and duplicated itself into two heterosexual counterparts of the male and the female. The production culminated into the reproductive system and the rule of bifurcation then gripped the process of fertilization of the cells in the embryo.

The scriptures bear ample testimony to this process of bifurcation of the original primary organism.

The *Brihadaranyak Upanishad*[3] narrates:

> "Earlier, the spirit personified was all alone and even on introspection found nothing other than

1. 10/129.
2. *Rigveda,* 10/121; *Yajurveda,* 31/1.
3. 1/4/1-3.

itself. In the beginning he said 'I am', and so he became 'I'; and so afterwards, when called on, he utters first of all that 'it is I' and thereafter tells his christened name.

'He was struck by fear and this explains why a lone man fears, and he brooded 'if there is no one other than I, who is that I am afraid of', and he was relieved of his fear.

'He could not conjugate. That is why the lone self cannot conjugate. He craved for another. He became clasped like male and female embraced. He split his body into two parts so as to become man and wife. Hence the body is unicorn blending the two petaloids of a single grain. Thus, the self realized its fullness. This conjugality led to the bearing of offsprings."

The *Manusmriti*[1] states:

"Dividing his body into two, he became a man with one-half and a woman with the other".

The description in the *Bible*[2] stating that "the rib which the Lord God had taken from man, made he a woman and brought her unto the man", is the same episode rhetorically worded a bit differently.

A more synchronized testimony on the point that the androgynous organism created the heterosexual race and itself perished, comes from Madam H.P. Blavatsky[3] and what she discovered can be summarized from her illustrative description as follows:

(i) Aristophanes speaks on the subject in Plato's *Banquet;*

1. 1/32.
2. Genesis, 2/22.
3. The Secret Doctrines, 1979, Adyar Edn., 1987 Reprint, II Vol., pp. 131-135.

"Our nature of old was not the same as it is now. It was androgynous, the form and the name partaking of, and being common to, both the male and the female....Their bodies were round and the manner of their running circular. They were terrible in force and strength and had prodigious ambition. Hence Zeus divided each of them into two, making them weaker; Apollo under his direction, closed up skin.

(ii) *Meshia* and *Meshiane* were but single individual with the old Persians. "They also taught that man was the product of the tree of life, growing in androgynous pairs, till they were separated as a subsequent modification of the human form.

(iii) In the *Book of Generations of Adam*, the verse "God created man in his own image, in the image of God created he him, male and female created he them," if read esoterically will yield the true sense, viz. "The Gods brought from themselves (by modification) man in their own image.... Created they him (collective humanity or Adam) male and female created he (collective deity) them....."

(iv) The sexless race was the first production, a modification of and from themselves, the pure spiritual existences and there was *Adam Solus*. Thence came the second race: *Adam-Eve* or *Yod-Havah,* inactive androgens; and finally the third or the "separating hermaphrodite", Cain and Abel, who produced the fourth, Seth-Enos. It is the fourth race tasted from the tree of good and evil, Eugibinus, a Christian, and the Rabbis Samuel, Mannasschben Israel and Maimoonides taught that "Adam had two faces and one person, and from the beginning, he was both male and female—male on one side and female on the other, like Manu's Brahma, but afterwards, the parts were separated, the one hundred and thirty-ninth Psalm of David is evidence of this. "Thou hast fashioned me behind and before", and the original word 'beset' is absurd and meaningless.

(v) So also in the Orphic hymns "Zeus was a male, Zeus was an immortal maid. The Egyptian Aman was the Goddess Neith, in his other half. Jupiter has female breasts. Venus is bearded in some of her statues; and Ila, the Goddess, is also Sudyumma, the God as Vaivaswat Manu's progeny.

(vi) It, therefore, follows that the first woman was formed subsequently to the first man, she must, as a logical necessity, have been taken out of man".

(vii) Thus, the third race is an axiom, and its virgin individuals were raised to 'Gods', because that race represented their dynasty. Mankind was evolved almost in a transparent condition of texture and neither by miracle and by sexual intercourse.

The androgynous theory is metaphysically more perfect in the Indian thought.

2. Perfect theory in Indian thought

The Indian thought has a more perfect picture of both extremes of the abstract and the concrete aspects of the androgynous theory.

As above so below, has been the realization of the great mystics and the seers. The distinction of appearance and reality has often been emphasised so that the enquiry may not lead the inquisitive mind to stop the search at the concrete which is after all phenomenal. The phenomenon, however, has always been treated as either the manifestation, production, emanation, creation, evolution or appearance of the noumenon. The noumenon is continuous with the phenomena and admits of no dividing line. The only distinction to be entertained is that of the gross and the subtle. The *Upanishads* steered clear in declaring the identity of the cosmos and the individual organism. The man is a miniature cosmos. Therefore, all human consciousness in its several aspects, knowing, feeling and willing, etc. at the individual level, are never individual but cosmic. All activities in the cosmos are the breaking vibrations of the one Absolute at the countless receptacles of individual existence. The *Purusha Sukta*[1] declares the whole creation as one infinite body. In the *Life Divine*[2], Sri Aurbindo remarks that there is no necessity in the essential nature of mind, sense or life, that they should be so limited; for physical sense organs are not creators of sense perception but themselves creation, and, hence, the conveyance of cosmic life force; the brain is not the creator of thought, but itself a creation, the instrument, and hence the necessary conveyance of cosmic mind. This necessity is not absolute, but biological; it is the result of the divine cosmic will in the material phenomenon.

The simple implication is that all life is one; and that One does exist. The crux of the thought is that life is one, uniform, continuous process.

The great seers visioned and intuited an Infinite space, an immense void or *Mahashunya* before the rise of the cosmic egg or the *Brahmanda*. A point was conceived within this great void, and that was the sexless state of

1. *Rigveda*, 10/90; *Yajurveda*, 31/1.
2. Vol. II, p. 391.

the infinite Being. In the *Purana* literature, which is both history and mythology, this boundless space was named as the *Aditi* which is the same as the seven-folded heaven in the Egyptian mysteries. The seers than visioned the point enlarging itself right and left, coalescent with the circumference and simulated a horizontal line like ——, and considered as the basal matter or the *Mula Prakriti*, or the primordial nature, so far virgin, and the seers thereafter conceived it as being crossed upon by a perpendicular line, which symbolized the nature being impregnated by the cosmic self. As a result, nature became vibrant to be geometrically signified as+, and this state symbolized the creation through the medium of sex. The term *Brahmanda* denoting the cosmic egg, also known as the *Hiranyagarbha*[1] implies the same theme. This *Hiranyagarbha* is an epicene bifurcated by its intensity into two, named respectively as the *Vach* and *Viraj*[2], that is the female and the male respectively.

The *Viraj*, the male counterpart, thus, split apart from the cosmic egg.[3] The word *Vach* which is the same thing as *Vak* denotes the *Saraswati*, deified in Hindu mythology as the Goddess of learning, the birth of which has been alluded to in the *Matsyapurana* as an off-shot from the *Brahma*, that is the entity pervading the *Brahmanda* or the cosmic egg. So, in the *Devi Bhagwat Purana*, the genesis of beings has been explained by the same process of bifurcation of one single entity into two.

The word *Vach* matches with its various synonyms as *Sandhya*, *Satrupa*, *Mula Prakriti*, *Savitri*, etc. with reference to her different contexts and relations, and is an aspect of the *Aditi* or the boundless. Similarly, *Brahma* is

1. *Rigveda*, 10/121.
2. *Manusmriti*, 1/32-33.
3. *Manusmriti*, 1/32.

another aspect of *Narain,* symbolizing the cosmic light. *Vach,* on the other hand, symbolizes the cosmic sound.

Science admits that the whole creation is nothing but the amalgam of light and sound in different degrees. In Indian linguistics, four kinds of sound are recognised, as the *Para,* the *Pashyanti,* the *Madhyama* and the *Vaikhari.* The first is the latent, absolute or the causal speech, the second is the vitality or the consciousness of speech, the third is silent speech and the fourth is conversational speech. On the same analogy, there is a parallel set of four kinds of light. The first the *Vaishwanar,* that is light on the earth perceived in the awakened state, the second that is *Pragya,* that which obtains in the state of dreams, corresponding to the light provided to the earth; the *Taijas,* which sustains the soul in the state of sleep, is the third, corresponding to the light surrounding the solar mass and the fourth, that is *Turiya,* is the light sustaining the regions above the solar system. The *Mandukya Upnishad* has referred to them in an esoteric way usual to the *Upanishads.*

Curiosity, of course, warrants an answer to the question why the unmanifest becomes manifest so as to turn the inaction into action. The plain answer in the *Rigveda*[1] is that inaction was metamorphosed into action, and the Being was rapt into becoming, because of its will, desire or instinct, denominated as the *Kama.* In Greek mythology, *Eros* was connected with the creation of the world which afterwards becomes the carnal Cupid. The Vedic character of *Kama* is not different. It is allegorically the psychic element developing the physiological features prior to the birth of the progenitor of the real biological race, known in the Hindu mythological lore as the *Prajapati,* or the Lord of the

1. 10/129.

Beings. Prior to the birth of the *Prajapati*, the creation was realized only through the will, the mental conation, of through sight or touch.

The generation of man came to its fruition only in the third towards the fourth race (cycle). The first and the second generations of beings were only mind-born, and the mind-born, bereft of flesh and bone, gave way to the will-born, equipped only with bones. This should have occurred in the middle of the third race which both philosophy and theology claim to be sexual and physiological, as has been succinctly accounted for also by *Madam Blavatsky* in her *Secret Doctrines*.

The creation in the beginning was sexless, developing thereafter into bisexuality and, finally, the male and the female came to be separated to become a sexual duality.

A pertinent point to be added is that the individual self, the *Atman* and the intellect, that is, the *Buddhi*, is mere duality which, when added with the mind or *manas*, becomes a triune. The *Kama*, that is, the will or the *Eros* is the seat of terrestrial and animal desire and passion. The first and the second races are of the nature of *Atman-Buddhi*, standing for the passive spiritual progeny, whereas the third root race shows three distinct divisions, psychologically and psychically, with the result that the earliest in the third race were sinless but the intermediate in this race were endowed also with the intelligence, and, therefore, prone to vice and virtue; and the last generation in this race becomes decidedly the animal being, where the mind or the *manas* becomes susceptible and vulnerable to temptation of sex in an abundant degree. In the two higher phases of this race, that is the self or the *Atman* and the intellect or the *Buddhi*, when subdued by mind, or the *manas*, the ego, needed as a fillip to terrestrial sensuous personality or the body. Thus, bereft of the personal will and egoistic desire, it would not have been possible to produce the human race endowed with individuality and manly personality.

Again, the *Kama* or the *Eros* in human beings has to depend on *Pran* or the life-breath, which is chemically the essence of blood. When the life-breath departs, the blood automatically congeals. The blood, therefore, is *Kamaroopa,* that is the sex-cum-form which pervades the whole body, and, the cerebellum is the *Kama* of the head, partially the central reservoir of all consciousness and concomitant conditions, functioning as the first-hand motivating force, and staying as the inherent cause of all creation latent in the cosmic personality, the Absolute or the *Virat Purusha.*

Creation starts with the stirring of *Kama* in the cosmic self; and it is this stirring or throbbing that throb after throb, the notions of space, time, and knowledge become comprehensible and assume prominence. The idea that primary deities in Egyptian and Christian mysteries were male and female simultaneously, cannot hence be discarded as fiction. In an Article[1], Alexander Wilder, of New York, maintained that the primeval race was double sexed. According to him, even now a large part of the vegetable creation, as well as animal kingdom, exhibits symptoms of bisexuality. In insect life, the moth generates a worm and the worm becomes a moth. The coral families reproduce, in Florida, from themselves, like the bud and ramifications in the trees. Bees are in the same line. Aristophanes, poet philosopher of Greece, in Plato's *Banquet,* stated that our nature of old was not the same as it is now, since it was androgynous, the form and the name partaking in and being common to both, the male and the female.[2]

1. The Theosophist, Feb., 1883, p. 112.
2. C H P Blavatsky; Secret Doctrines, 7th Adyar Edn., 1979, pp. 96, 133-134, 177.

The transcendental reality, in the Hindu ideal of the *Parabrahman*, which the Kabalists know as Ainsoph, is identified as the spirit that moves upon waters, *Manu Swayambhuvah*, literally meaning as the self-born, the *Adam-Kodman* of the *Kabalists* and the Androgyne man of *Genesis*-I, are identical. *Adam-Kodman*, in the *Genesis*[1] separated himself into two halves, male and female, becoming *Jah-Hovah* or *Jehorab-Eve*, in same fashion as the Hindu deity *Brahma* became *Viraj-Vach*. All such mystic notions are not farce but cosmic facts.

The process of creation is evinced from the sexless stage to the bi-sexual level, and from the latter, to the sexual state. In an urge to comprehend the mighty generator of the universe, man has no alternative but to symbolise. The female womb is the microscopic copy and reflection of the Heavenly Matrix, the female that is, the space energy, in which the male spirit fecundates the germ of the species as have become visible in the universe.

In Hindu mythology, the point of bifurcation has been minutely investigated and miraculously depicted in the image of the *Ardhanarishwar* which is half-man and half-woman, the epicene, denoting the hermaphrodite stage of the reality at large, a far primitive stage when the bifurcation of Eros into sexes was labouring fast to become manifest. The last terminus of the naked Adam and Eve, has been conceived in the mere distinction of the respective male and female organs, and save the specified two ocular genital organs, there is no conspicuous dissimilarity in the male and the female bodies. Naturally, therefore, the interaction, that is, the sordid or the formidable incident of penetration, could be feasible through the organs set opposite to each other in

1. *Verse* 2.

contrast but compromising positions. In the esoteric image of the *Ardhanarishwar,* the two bodies being in full length, the diameter for bifurcation had to be underlined. In the last factual art what was important was not the line of bifurcation but the exercise facilitating the reunion of two bodies for purpose of enjoying each other. In the fulfillment of this mission of creation, as depicted in the *Brihadaranyak Upnishad*[1], what can necessarily be emphasised is the two magnetic points of polarity whereon the male and the female could react and reciprocate.

The thought, therefore, concentrates on the bare act of cohabitation and the same was concretized in the symbol of the *Shivalinga,* the phallus planted in the vagina, which, for sake of clear visibility, was the reverse of phallus penetrated into the vagina, and the worship of the phallus and the vagina in union became a prominent cult.

These two symbols tell the evolution, or, in other words, the deployment of *Kama* into sex. This deployment is often termed degeneration or downfall. The fall of *Adam* is descent of the cosmic Eros into the mundane sex. Obviously, therefore, there can be nothing about the method or technique explaining the stages prior to the origin of mammalia. The consummation of *Kama* gets complex in what *Shivalinga* stands for, and the *Ardhanarishwar* or the epicene concept of the Being gets personified into the man and the woman united in action.

Man, as such, discovered the divine piety in phallic worship as reverence to the pious act of creation. The Hindus had this simple exoteric idea of worshipping and paying obeisance to the *Shiva lingam* representing the

---

1. 1/4/3.

spirit erect in the female vagina, the *yoni* of mother of *Parvati* which represents the *Prakriti* or the Mother Nature.

This form of worship was misunderstood by snobs as an epitome of indecency but such criticism was retorted back by Madam H. P. Blavatsky[1] saying:

> "We find it rather unwise on the part of Catholic writers to pour out their vials of wrath in such sentences as these: *In a multitude of pagodas, the phallic stone, ever and always assuming, like the Grecian bactylos, the brutally indecent form of the linga....the Mahadeva.* Before casting slurs on a symbol whose profound metaphysical meaning is too much for the modern champions of that religion of sensualism *par excellence.* Roman Catholicism, to grasp, they would have been duty bound to destroy their oldest churches, and change the form of the Cupolas of their own temples. The *Mahadev* of Elephanta, the round tower of Bhagalpur, the minarets of Islam—either rounded or pointed, are the originals of the Campanile column of San Marco at Venice, of Rochester Cathedral, and of the modern Duomo of Milan. All of these steeples, turrets, domes and christian temples, or the reproductions of the primitive idea of the *Lithos,* the upright phallus."

Madam Blavatsky[2] refers to the following account from the Zabar, the mystic compositions of the Hebrew Kabalists:

> "The pre-Adamite kings. We have learned in the Siphrah D' Tznioothah: That the At-tee' kah D' At tee'keen, Ancient of Ancients, before He prepared

1. The Secret Doctrines, 1979 Adyar Edn., Vol. II, p. 85
2. *Ibid,* pp. 82-84.

> His Form, built kings, and engraved kings, and sketched out kings [men, the Kings of the animals], and they could not exist: till He overthrew them *and hid them until after a time,* therefore it is written: "And these are the kings which reigned in the land of Edom".....And they could not exist till *Resha Hiv'rah,* the White Head, the At-tee-'kah D' At-tee'keen, Ancient of the Ancients, arranged Himself......formed all forms Above and Below.......Before He arranged Himself in His Form, had not been formed all those whom He desired to form, and all worlds have been destroyed.....they did not remain in their places, because the form of the kings had not been formed as it ought to be, and *the Holy City had not been prepared."*

Interpreting the concepts involved in the above passage Madam Blavadsky states:

> "Before man could become male and female physically, his prototype, the creating Elohim, had to arrange his form on the sexual plane astrally. That is to say, the atoms and the organic forces, descending into the plane of the given differentiation, had to be marshaled in the order intended by nature, so as to be ever carrying out, in an immaculate way, that law which the *Kabala* called the Balawee, through which every thing that exists does so as male and female in its final perfection, in this present stage of materiality. Hokhamah, wisdom, the male Sephiroth, had to diffuse itself in and through Binah, intelligent nature, or understanding. Therefore, the first Root Race of man, sexless and mindless, had to be overthrown and hidden until after a time, i.e., the first race instead of dying disappeared in the

> second race as certain lower lives and plants do in their progeny. It was a wholesale transformation. The first became the second Root Race, without their begetting it, procreating or dying. They passed by together, as is written: He died and another reigned in his stead. Why? Because the Holy City had not been prepared. And what the Holy City? The Maquom (the secret place or the shrine) on earth: in other words, the human womb, the microscopic copy and reflection of the Heavenly Matrix, the female space or primeval chaos, in which the male spirit fecundates the germ of the son, or the visible universe."

Supporting the Hindu thought, Madam Blavadsky concludes:

> ".....the fact that all these Hebrew Elohim, sparks and cherubs are identical with the Devas, Rishis and the Fires and Flames, the Rudras and the forty-nine *Agnis* of the ancient *Aryas,* is sufficiently proven by and in the Kabala."

The names, that is, the *Devas, Rishis, Rudras,* and *Agnis* which are Fires or Flames, are terms of art, irrelevant to their literal meanings, and as sparks of life, denote the sources or generators of life. In the *Rigveda*[1], it is stated that all these generators of life, have been moulded by *Brahmanspati,* which is an esoteric name representing the cosmic manufactor, on the analogy of the blacksmith moulding his wares by working at his bellows.

Thus the name *Brahmanspati,* may not be omnipotent or omniscient in the absolute sense of the term, but certainly connotes, in the context, the great designer, or simply, the builder or the mason, working under the

1. 10/72.

impulse given to him by the ever-to-be unknown, Master that is, the cosmic spirit or the universal soul, law and life involved in one. It is just matter of surmise, with no accuracy of data needed for its proof, that this mason or manufactor, can have a hand or choice or possibility of working out or producing patterns specifically warranted for the particular cycle of creation, and the patterns are worked out on a strictly geometrical scale of progression, degression, or even digression, thus, in the creation of any new pattern, for the species, departing spontaneously, sometimes very differently, from the parent stock, and as in the great variety of the genus felis, that is the feline species of the lynx, cat, tiger, etc. it is the impulse of the designer either to add to or deprive any given species of certain appendages needed or becoming needless in the new set of clime or environment.

The exegesis made above and as hithertobefore, must affirm certain simple but irreversible conclusions.

3. Certain, simple, irreversible conclusions

3.1 The Reality as One-in-Two

The primordial reality is one but capable of dualising itself. It is, therefore, two-in-one which is inherently a force or vitality, the seers have ascribed different names, each as synonym of the other, like will, impulse, Eros or conation. All force destined to deploy itself into action, inevitably assumes unto itself a duality. Behind each action, there is a force implied and the curious feature of this esoteric entity of force is that even after its deployment in action after action, it never gets exhausted. The doer deploys his force in one action and remains capable of deploying the same force, in varying degrees, into an unending series of actions. The action is mere manifest effect of deployment of force, and in becoming manifest, the factual activity represents its original force. Taking a stock example, a duelist in himself is a force concentrated, even when if is not engaged in a duel, yet capable anytime, of duelling. Thus, in simple polemics, the force as an entity as also a capacity to spring into action, are logically two-in-one. Thus, the will concentrated in the reality to manifest and the capacities to manifest are essentially one but virtually two. The seers thus visualized a point of bifurcation of the force into a faculty and a capacity; and this bifurcation is not actual bi-section but a notional duet; and since the process of creation once started, continues incessantly, and unabated, the force and the action are liable to throughout remain intervolved and interactive, unlike the duelist who duels at times and is otherwise in a state of rest, whereas the creation is one continuous activity until it reaches its destiny in its dissolution.

The reality or the unmanifest stage having no physical frame, the bifurcation connotes nothing more than its diversion into two streams meant for materializing and forging ahead the process as originally connived so that the two streams can react and interact, without forfeiting the fundamental unity at bottom; and it is this fundamental unity which forfends against their total alienation and compels, on the other and, their reciprocation, each containing in varying proportion the content of the other, because the process of one becoming many cannot fructify without initially becoming two. **It is neither knowledge nor faith but mathematical or logical necessity of monism to assume dualism to beget into pluralism.** If the one after becoming two were conceived as total alienation or absolute, isolation, there could be no chance of cooperation with each other. The inherent instinct of unity impels them to unite and act in unison to issue forth into myriads. If the two were independent and forlorn, it would be denial of their impulse to unite in any event and at any cost.

As an aftermath of such bifurcation, the one stream stands for cosmic sentience, called by whatever name, as the spirit, the *Purusha* or the soul, and the other as cosmic action, dynamicity, the matter or the *Prakriti*. **Processes after processes of alchemy in the cosmic foundry, the involution of the two currents become forged into epicenic entities to descend down by force of space energy, to thrust into the follicles of the earth for the final breakthrough into a hermaphrodite organism to facilitate, in due course, their actual and physical bifurcation.**

The concept of Two-in-One may be mystery but is neither conundrum nor fallacy but a simple manoeuvres of the Will. In order to create, there must be a substance for being created. In order to make, there has to be matter to be made out from; and the will to create is followed by the matter emanating from the spirit. It is an automatic breakthrough of the material cause from the efficient cause.

3.2 Breakthrough of Material from Spiritual

The *Upnishad*[1] has explained the emanation of the material cause from the efficient cause in simple affable terms, same that just as the spider creates the yarn for its cobweb out of its own belly without any external aid and gulps it again at its will, so the cosmic self or the *Purush*, issues forth the cosmic matter or the *Prakriti* out of itself for conjuring up the cosmic scene. Another analogy employed by the *Upnishad* to explain the same phenomenon is that just as the bones, hairs, teeth and the nails grow out automatically from the embryo, so is the case of generation of the matter out of the spirit itself.

It is this art of conjuring up the show out of itself, just as the wizard creates a variety of ocular things out of the

1. *Mundakopnishad*, 1/1/7.

vacuity, and they are real so long as they are visible. "And God said, let their be light, and there was light", is the same explanation in the *Genesis,* or the emanation of the material cause out of the efficient cause. It is on the simulation of this conjuration that the Vedantins call it as *Maya* or an apparent illusion.

Why after all the spider would generate the glutinous substance from its own vitals to spin out a yarn for its web, is question impossible of an exoteric answer for any religion or philosophy, except that it is an inevitable execution of its instinct; and the answer in the Hindu thought is verily not different. The *Rigveda*[1] accepts the theory of the cosmic libido, or the *Kama* as the indomitable will or the invincible vibrating force of the Cosmic Being. It does so for its own sport or recreation, a fun or fancy, as explained in the *Brahmasutras* by employing the term *Leela,* or thaumaturgy, aptly called by the Vedantins as the *Maya;* and since it is done at will, and since the will betokens the life principle, the generation from the spirit of its material counterpart is a concentrate of life. It is the momentous event of egress of life, though this life principle has yet to traverse a number of other stages to become real animate life.

The initial stuff emancipated from the spirit is the space energy, which the Hindu cosmology calls as the *aakash,* the ether being its nearest synonym, which is life in its subtlest form. The *aakash* generates the air, comparatively a grosser form of *aakash;* the air generates fire, comparatively a grosser manifestation of air; the fire generates water, again a grosser transformation of fire; and, finally, the water turns into its grossest manifestation in the form of Earth. The Earth produces the herbs, the herb becomes corn; and it is from the corn

1. 10/129.

that an organism is born[1] and becomes the real receptacle of mundane life. These five principles, in their gradual grosser manifestations, are, therefore, termed in the Hindu cosmoslogy as the *Bhutas* or the elements or the ingredients of the *Prakriti* at large.

The *Prakriti,* which is nature, or the matter or the materiality at large, cannot be comprehended without inherent peculiar heterochromous characteristics. The emanation of matter which is the material cause, from the *Purusha* which is spirit and the efficient cause, is not partition but only counterparting. **The spirit in the matter is just mate or match to each other, the former as dominant and the latter as servient. Both are alter egos for each other.**

Again, the known evolutes of nature, namely, the *aakash,* air, fire, water and earth, are neither sections or sectors but ingredients of nature, in the same way as sentiènce, ego, knowledge or mind are ingredients of the spirit. The *aakash,* which in the Hindu cosmology is not a void or space alone but space and substance compact and that being the first manifest evolute of matter, conserves within itself the property of the rest of the four elemental evolutes of air, fire, water and earth, and likewise, each of the rest of these elements being effects of *aakash* are never without their basic content of *aakash.* The nature is five-in-one, capable of becoming either, by force of the concussions on it of the dominant spirit. The *aakash,* the air, the fire, the water and the earth are not defined or delineated areas or belts of the nature but only its gradual subsidences and when dissolved or caused to dissolve finally, must repose in the very first evolute of *aakash;* and this is just a phenomenal complex, but being counterpart of the spirit, the nature is not without its

---

1. *Taittiriya Upanishad,* 2/1.

psychic spell. In its synergy with the spirit, it represents itself into definite declinations; and these declinations classified in the Hindu ethology into three ethical orders.

The so called classification need not be misconceived, again, as distinct vestibules of nature. These are rather variable versions of nature committed and corresponding to human nature. They can aptly be described as modes of nature or the modalities in which the cosmic nature manifests itself into the human nature. This explains the difference in the meaning of 'nature' with reference to the cosmos and the individual self. **In relation to the cosmos, the word 'nature' connotes the cosmic materiality at large, that is, the material cause, but in relation to mankind, the word nature refers to the innate moral fibre in particular man.**

In the Hindu philosophy, the modes, or more correctly, the frequencies of nature have been named as the *Sattva,* the *Rajas* and the *Tamas,* as adjectively standing respectively for the superlative, the comparative and the lowest grade in persons and things.

The *Sattva* stands for the virtuous, the *Rajas* represent the Voluptuous and the *Tamas* can be conceived as the worst, the lowest, the meanest or the vilest. The first one is perfection *par excellence.* The second denotes passions in men. The third comprehends, in terms, all that is philosophically conceived as evil. The trash and condemned characters in the social ethos are possessed mostly by the third mode of *Tamas.* The common mediocre men are neither wholly puritan nor thoroughly fallen. They are capable as much of doing fine acts as of committing foibles. They are destined to the second mode, of the *Rajas.* They are indulgent as well as abstinent. They represent the hybrid of the *Tamas* and the *Sattva.* The *Sattva* is top nature which is spiritual perfection perhaps attained or attainable by sages, saints and philanthropists. They are institutions of the sociality, the morality and the spirituality. They are servants of God and serviceable to society and humanity in general.

With what mode of its own, the nature would endow any particular life, may be difficult to predict or prelect except with reference to the vexatious principle of the Hindu ethics known as the *law of Karma*. What is relevant is that the nature chooses its own course and comes to dwell in particular life in its chosen proportion of its three modes, called in the *Samkhya* philosophy, and anywhere in the Hindu naturology, as the three aforesaid *Gunas*, that is, the modes or frequencies. Any mode can vest in any life in any proportion and there can be no external intervention in this proportionality. The moment the nature is let loose into process, the spirit assumes life and the mode of nature captures it in its destined proportion. The whole cosmos, on this event of unification of spirit and nature, is filled with life. **The spirit covets the nature and the nature clamps upon it in its proportioned modes** and stays throughout as the determinant of the trait of behavior of the self in any life. The cosmos is one reservoir of life, with the inherent variance therein in accordance with which in the amalgam of its three modes any particular chunk of life had come to be dominated by, without in any way affecting the integrality of the life principle as a whole, in the same way as the different and distracted currents on the surface of the sea do not cause any upheaval in its depth. **Life comes down on Earth from the cosmic space and recants to the same cosmic space on its dissolution.** The process is recurring and explains the cycle of births and deaths.

3.3 *The cycle of births and deaths*

The Upanishads have explained this recurrence of life and death with meticulous coherence.

The life has its roots in the yonder heavens, says the *Kath Upnishad*[1] and the *Gita.*[2] Human life has its root above and its branches down. The *Brihadaranyak*[3] and the *Chhandogya Upanishads*[4] *have* given a systematic and logical account of the advent of life from the cosmic space down to the Earth in five consecutive downward stages. The *Upanishads* have ascribed the process to the interplay of the cosmic energy at five consequent levels of its cadency.

The agency responsible for carnification of cosmic life has been denominated as the fire with all its attributes and incidents. The advent of life is revered as a pious cosmic ritual; and the fires at work on five levels have been named as five rounds of oblations into the corresponding fires deployed at each level. Giving credence to the consuming nature of fire, the five-fold deployment of cosmic energy has been rightly named as the five alternations of fire. The process denotes a perfect science which the *Upnishads* designate as the science of five fires (*Panchagni Vidya*).

3.4 Science of Five Fires

In the first round, the heavenly region itself serves as basic fire. The Sun is natural fuel. The rays of the Sun are the smoke. The diurnal horae are the flames. The Moon is the ember and the stars are the sparks. In this fire the cosmic forces pour the *Shraddha* as oblation which generates the *Soma.*

The terms *Sharddha* and *Soma* are terms of art and replete with a number of connotations. *Shraddha* literally means an intermediate between faith and adoration. The *Soma* literally stands for the Moon or, some times, the

1. 2/3/1.
2. 15/1.
3. 6/2.
4. 5/4-9.

nectar. In the metaphysical sense, and with reference to the element of fire, it is a surrogate name for any fuel. What the *Upanishads* mean is that the element of Moon serves as constant fire to the burning Sun. The *Soma* poured into the Sun keeps the reactor of the Sun constantly burning and the burnt *Soma* is again sprayed into the space and the process continues with the *Soma* pouring in and the fire of Sun always kept burning. Since the *Soma* has itself to be a substance, the Upanishads contemplated another subtle substance as the root and cause of *Soma* itself. Conceivably, **the *Shraddha* can refer to a substance emitted off the Sun as a result of burning of the *Soma* substance.** Finally, *Shraddha* itself stands for the basic or fundamental fuel for energizing the cosmic play.

It would be futile exercises to find the exact equivalents of these terms in the English vocabulary. With reference to the context, they represent the chemical subtleties of the cosmos in their antecedent and consequent forms of composition. Since these are the basic ingredients of the life stuff, the word *Shraddha* may well represent the ether. The word refers to the first chemical of the cosmos which is naturally the ether. The ether is content of *aakash* which is the first product of the material reality known in the Hindu scriptures as the *Prakriti*.

The word *Soma* is, thus, a substance derived after the celestial processing of solar energy and can be taken as the lunar energy.

The Sun is the cosmic reactor. In order to keep it aflame, there is constant requirement of fuel. The ether in the *aakash* supplies that need.

The flame, the embers, the sparks and the smoke are normal incidents of the activity of burning and are, therefore, described without any figurative implication, as incidents of any fire.

The fuel consumed by fire is turned into coal, ash and smoke. True that where there is smoke, there is fire, but truer it is that where there is fire, there has to be smoke. It is only the gross and hard stuff of the fuel which turns into coal or ash, but in case the fuel is soft and subtle, there is no question of any excretion in the form of coal or ashes, and the fuel, when consumed assumes a gaseous form, so as to be directly dissolved into the air. If wood is supplied as fuel to any fire, it is liable to display its activity in all the incidence of flames, embers, sparks and smoke, but if butter is poured into fire, it becomes flame and finally turns into vapour. The ether being a fine, subtlemost substance, is consumed in the reactor of the Sun and leaves neither sediment nor excretion. It assumes at once a gaseous form and is dissolved again, within no time, into the *aakash* and is converted at once into ether. This constant activity of ether falling into the reactor and its instant reversion into the *aakash*, validates the unabating process without the least diminution whether of the fuel or of the fire, and both subsist conterminously till eternity.

In the second process of the fire, the rain is the fire; the year is its fuel, the cloud is the smoke, the lightning is the flame; the thunder is the ember, the roar of the cloud is spark; and in that fire *Soma*, the by-product of the first round, when poured in, causes the rainfall.

In the second round, the lunar energy is, thus, liquefied into the rain water.

In the third round, the terrestrial region is the fire; the Earth is its fuel, the day is the smoke, the night is the flame, the Moon is the ember and the stars are sparks; and in this fire, the rain water is poured; and the cereal is born.

In this third round, the *Soma* of the first round is transformed into the corn. The *anna* or the cereal is, therefore, one among several meanings ascribed to the term *Soma*.

In the fourth round, the male serves as the fire; the gap of his mouth serves as the fuel, the life breath is the smoke, the speech is the flame, the eyes are embers; the ears are sparks; and the corn digested in the stomach generates the semen.

In this fourth round, the grain, the by-product of the third round, is reprocessed into the semen which is the seed of the embryo.

In the final, fifth round, the female is the fire, her genital organ is the fuel, the bristles serve as smoke, the vagina is the flame, the cohabitation is the ember, the orgasm denotes the sparks; and in this fire, the semen is inseminated and this makes up a live person.

The fifth round is the culmination of the life process and the astral or the ethereal life principle becomes life incarnate; and the process from the first to the fifth is sequence natural and infallible.

The reason why carnified life comes to be fabricated only at the fifth level, is not obscure. The space energy on the above four levels cannot sustain carnalised life because of their comparatively higher degrees of calefaction. The fires from the first to the fourth levels become gradually milder and lubricated, and it is only at the fifth level that the heat comes down to a level fit to sustain life. It is only when the heat comes down to the level merely of warmth that life can subsist. Since life can subsist only at a specified temperature, it is utterly impossible for carnalised life to stay at comparative levels of incineration obtaining at the above four levels.

This comprobates the fact that the cosmos though throughout filled with life, the same is in terms of a different sort, may be of psychic spiritual, astral, aural or penumbric forms, and becomes carnified in its gradual descent only at the fifth stage. The outer and higher space is the only abode of life, or more correctly, of the life principles or modes of life.

There is yet a sixth round of fire which serves as the intermedium evincing the recurrent process of births, deaths and re-births.

The *Upnishad*[1] states that so long as life survives within a particular frame of body, it performs its given activities and when captured by death, the mortal frame is consigned to the funeral fire and in the process of its consumption by that fire, all the incidents of life spark revert to their original ingredients. The fire dissolves into the cosmic fire; the fuel returns to the cosmic incandescence, the smoke recants to the cosmic gaseousness; the flames defuse into its corresponding rays; the embers retreat into their cosmic contents and the sparks regain their corresponding cosmic property.

Consequent on death, life returns to the same cosmic space whence it had descended down on Earth. The Upnishad narrates the process of re-birth.

3.5 The Process of Re-birth

The departed soul endures a fixed period in yonder space, and what and how such period is destined, is attributable to the same formidable principle known as the Law of Karma.

The *Upnishad*[2] states that after exhausting his destined period in the outer space, the departed souls return by traversing the same process, by initially

1. *Brihadaranyak*, 6/2/14.
2. *Chhandogya*, 5/10/5-6.

assuming an ethereal form, and, from that, they come down into the aerial form.

Thereafter they assume the carbonic or penumbric form and thenceforth they are taken into the cloudy mass to thereafter metamorphose into the rain and fall down in drops and then grow out as corn, cereal, herb or flora, and **whosoever consumes that stuff and emits the semen processed from such food through ejaculation, is finally turned into the corresponding embryo typical to the species which had taken up that particular edible.**

A question has been posed both in the *Chhandogya*[1] and the *Brihadaranyak*[2] Upanishads—why the cosmic space does not become overcrowded by the souls departing after death from the terrestrial region and, similarly, why the terrestrial region, too, does not get overcrowded by those re-born on Earth. The process delineated above satisfies both these questions. **The life of the dead goes up to the heavenly space and the same again comes down to the Earth, so as to maintain the recurrent balance here as well as hereafter.**

The recent study on meteorites confirms the concept that life on Earth has come down from cosmic space.

4. Study of Meteorites

The recent findings that life on Earth came through meteorites are based on a study of a meteorite that fell in the State of Rajasthan, in India, in 1991, which contained amino acids and bacteria.

Prof. B. S. Paliwal, the Dean of the Faculty of Science, and Head of Department of Geology at the Jai Narain Vyas University, Jodhpur (India), believes that life might have originated in outer space and not on Earth.

1. 5/3/3.
2. 6/2/2.

Subsequently, life was transferred to the Earth through comet dust and meteorite showers. Prof. Paliwal believes that evolutionary stages in the history in the life on Earth are due to the impact of extra-terrestrial bodies on Earth from time to time. Professor Paliwal, had presented a paper in the 32nd International Geological Congress (IGC) held in Florence, Italy, which commence on August 20, 2004.

Mathew A. Pasck, a doctoral candidate in the Planetary Science at the University of Arizona, has substantially shared the same view that different phosphorus compounds in meteorites are responsible for sustainability of life on Earth.

Prof. Paliwal found it interesting to note that at the Crambian time, trilolites vanished but, on the other hand, corals and crinoids proliferated, and when dinosaurs became extinct about sixty five million years ago, mammals and delicate fishes proliferated, thus, creating doubt about Darwin's theory of evolution.

Prof. Paliwal rightly held that the five gross elements of natures, namely, the sky, the air, the fire, the water and the Earth have played an important role in the formation of life, and, out of these, the sky, that is the *aakash*, must mean the outer space, has its prominent role in the formation of the life.

Prof. Paliwal, had noticed these amino acids, namely phenylalanine, tyrosine and tryptopham, for the first time in the D-R meteorite that fell near Didwana in Nagour Distt., in 1991. The discovery got acceptance when the findings of Prof. Paliwal were published in the Journal of Geological Society of India.

Soon after the fall of meteorite, Prof. Paliwal, conducted his study on its composition and his finding, showed that the meteorite in question was very much different from others. Prof. Paliwal referred to two theories about the origin of life on the Earth: one, suggesting that life originated on the planet, and the other, that is, it was brought on Earth from outer space by meteoroids.

Amino acids are the building blocks of life and their presence in the meteorite suggested that organic components were derived form proto-planets.

Prof. Paliwal referred to the Laser Raman Spectroscopic studies of the meteorite which confirmed presence of aromatic acids in the acids components of meteorites.

Sh. Vinod Tiwari of the Wadio Institute of Himalayan Geology at Deharadun, has also carried out experiments on this meteorite, and corroborated that the amino acids found in the D-R meteorites were extra-terrestrial and his analysis ruled out any ground contamination.

The veracity of the meteorite theory is interesting though acceptable only in part.

5. Meteorite Theory Partly Acceptable

That life on Earth has come from cosmic space is perennial faith of the Vedic cosmology. In the *Kathopnishad*[1] and in the *Bhagwadgita*[2] the tree of life is stated to have its roots above and stem down; and the statement has only metaphorised the affirmation that the cosmic spaces is replete with life and life on Earth comes from cosmic space. The five elements of natures, namely, the *aakash*, the air, the fire, the water, and the earth exist in their subtle and elementary forms in the cosmic space. The Earth may be grossest elemental substance, solidified in course of time from its causal content in the outer

1. 2/3/1.
2. 15/1.

space which holds and retains all the vital contents of life. The material content of the Earth is a boon of cosmic space. The meteorite, too, has come from the outer space, and there is nothing strange in the meteorite containing the basic ingredients of life; and the amino acid discovered in the fallen meteorite is evidence of its deposit in the meteorite from the vaporous hydraulic content present in the cosmic space. The star or the planet wherefrom the meteorite severed itself from its parent body was itself lodged in the outer space. **It is, therefore, one thing to say that the meteorite contains the germs of life but quite another to maintain that life on Earth had come through the meteorite. The Earth itself has its origin from outer space.**

The statement that following the extinction on Earth of the whole race of dinosaurs, delicate fishes proliferated, has no basis to deny the existence of the aquatic species even in or before the *Jurassic Age.*

That after (or before) extinction of the Jurassic race, the delicate fishes proliferated, is nothing new to the Hindu cosmology.

The one single source of energy that becomes life, comes from the Sun, which is in the Hindu mythology is a synonym of *Vishnu,* and each life on Earth is rightly ascribed to the incarnation of *Vishnu.* A cell composed of the amino acid, that with a nucleus, when allows the Sun beam to pierce through it, becomes life representing its corresponding pre-existent pattern of life in the outer space, and it is life in the outer space which evolves into higher and newer forms.

The scriptures have depicted the successive incarnations, named as *avatars,* of the Sun. What is depicted is the transformation of a single cell developed into the ocean and finally evolving into complex structure of man adopting the basic pattern from outer space. The Hindu series of epics, named each as a *Purana* bear testimony to these events.

Beginning from the sea life, because the first incident of energy transforming into life, is represented into the pisces family, is the *Matsya Avatar* of *Vishnu* or the incarnation of the Sun into the fish. The second round of aquatic life is the tortoise or the *Kurma Avatar* of *Vishnu,* which is aquatic life with a hard cluster, and, therefore, a development of the first, and thereafter the pig or the *Varaha;* and, thenceforth, the Lion, the *Narsingha,* the sphinx, and finally, the man, though initially in a dwarfish form, that is, the *Vamana;* and it was never an ape but the human dwarf which latter developed into a full human form.

There have been millions and millions of processes in between these stages, and it was feasible only to underline the prominent stages, ignoring the other minute and miscellaneous or intermediate details and the intervening processes.

These details in the *Purana* literature, that is, epic literature of the Hindus, have depicted the development of the fish into the tortoise which is a more complex structure of its predecessor, the fish. The epics had discarded the necessity of tracing all the species in their order of succession, which in the Hindu mythological surmises, has a numerical strength of eighty-four lacs, which again may not be exact but only a device to assert the innumerability of the species. It was convenient only to name only the significant few, and, therefore, the epics took a leap from the tortoise direct to the peculiar species of a hybrid type, having the head of a man fixed on the torso of a lion, becoming the *Narsingha* or the leoman, and thence proceeded to take into account the *homo sapien,* originally in its short statured dwarfish form.

literally meaning *Vamana* or the homunculus which naturally, and in course of time, must have become evolved into its manly size by nourishment and ongoing natural processes and physical exertion.

There have been others in the hybrid kind, for example, the *Ganesha,* having a human torso juxtaposed to the head of an elephant, or the *Hayagreeva,* that is the neck and head of a horse assembled on the torso of man. Such anomalous creatures, rare as they had been, and if their origin be not altogetherly a myth, can be explained, in the absence of no tangible evidence of their factual existence in real life, by ascribing their origin to a queer freak of nature or an accidental error of mislaying to incompatible orders of life, but **since such species were not known to have begotten their like, they are definitely out of the line of approved forms of life; and because of their bizarre appearance, they must have instilled in the viewers some sense of sublimity and awe, and eventually became objects of adoration or worship; and because of their incompetence to multiply their stock, they stayed in the human reminiscence as unique gifts of nature.** Such accidental mis-combination of two different orders of life cannot, however, be ruled out.

That life may or should have an aquatic origin may neither be doubted nor discarded. The vegetative life, which is the staple food of the mammalia itself, owes its origin to water. **The botanical sustains the zoological life;** and, otherwise, the complex life must have succeeded their preceding simpler forms. The amino acids are themselves the by-product of water; and none can doubt that water itself comes from outer space. Even the in-depth water underground can have no other source except from the outer space; Water pours from outer space on planes of Earth, and is the cause of formation of the amino acids much in the same way as in any other planet, unless it is proved that there is no rainfall on any other solar satellite. If the corpulent lump of Earth were bumped up into the outer space so as to deposit on any planet, the result should have been not different than that of the meteorite falling on Earth from some planet which could not yet generate life on his parent mass despite its life content. Life in its causal essence permeates the cosmos through and through. **The temporal life, or the life incarnate is the culmination of the life principle throughout infused in the cosmos with the result that life patterns or forms or designs of life are first projected in the ethereal space.**

6. Forms or Patterns of Life

The cosmic space, thus, provides for centres of creative power for every root or parent life patterns of the host of forms of botanical or zoological life; and each pattern is a generalized design worked out by the cosmic designer. These centres contain a specific germ or spark of life, and can be conceived as the cosmic mason or manufactor. The statement in the *Rigveda*[1] names these designers as *Brahmanspati*, busy with moulding the life forms just as a blacksmith works out at his bellows the molten iron into desired wares; and each builder builds the whole race of its form on design set by itself; and it is no wonder that gradual improvements, modifications, deviations or departures from the basic or inherent form, may occur accidentally, since flaws are incidental to any practical process. The result is that **in the whole Nature at work in an absolute space, there can be billions and billions of different and different patterns altogetherly incompatible to each other. And, there are uncountable life principles or centres of life which are at work, each**

1. 10/72.

against others, and a multiplicity of forms or patterns is very much usual, in the same way as that of a smith at work making out different and dissimilar wares out of the same stuff.

Genesis of life is spontaneous, as a premium of the initial coalescence of spirit and matter, that is the *Purusha* and the *Prakriti.* Life is generated *en masse* so as to permeate, at the first hand, in the entire cosmic space. **Life being an active, dynamic process, it cannot rest idle but gets into the process of modifying and sampling itself into classic archetypes.**

The *Vishnu Purana*[1] denominates these archetypes as Mind Born. They were the first progeny of the cosmic progenitor named as *Brahma.* These Mind Born entities were without desire or passion but inspired with holy wisdom. Naming them as nine in the first edition of the Mind Born, the *Vishnu Purana* describes them as analogous to their progenitor or bearer.

The statement in the Purana is that when the progeny of the progenitor could not evolve in the line of sons and grandsons, the progenitor brought forth *Bhrigu, Pulastya, Pulah, Kriti, Angira, Marichi, Daksh, Atri, and Vashishtha,* all in ilk as himself. The *Purana* literature recognises these nine as primal progenitors. Thereafter, they produced *Khyati, Bhooti, Sambhooti, Kshama, Preeti, Samaty, Oorja, Anasuya* and *Prasuti,* as the nine virgins and told them to become consorts for the above nine progenitors.

The Purana proceeds to state that from the wrath of the prime progenitor another life came out as *Rudra* and it was this formidable personage of this tenth Mind Born, which combined into itself two bodies, half man and half woman. The progenitor commanded him to bifurcate

---

1. 1/7/3-15.

himself into two different bodies of the male and the female. Ultimately these two male and female originals divided themselves into different progenies.

There is no magic in the names cited in the *Purana,* and any name was as good as another. It is just compulsion of description to coin some nomenclature for any anthropomorphic entity for distinction and identity.

Even otherwise, each Samskrit word has its etymological meaning traced to its original root; and much as the names might be fancied, the number of nine, too, is fancied as the highest in numerology.

Each scripture has its own way of narrating events and it is natural to be esoteric, figurative and rhetoric. No mortal being could ever behold the real genesis of the cosmos; and the subject itself being ineffable, some degree of catharsis and synecdoche is inevitable; and the version of the seers has to be logically interpreted and their linguistic implication has to be meticulously deciphered. **If the theory of bifurcation is resorted to unanimously in several scriptures and the fact that the first root race was hermaphrodite, cannot be dented or defied, there can, then, otherwise, be no explanation for the bisexual race.** Thus, space or *aakash* being the first cosmic product, it cannot be denied, without doing violence to commonsense, that all creative process must have followed as events in sequence in the space, and must have finally become incarnate on Earth after so many cyclic processes traversing epochnating eras, which the Hindu scriptures have named as *Manvantaras.* The word *Manvantara* denotes the interlude between the series of existentiality counted to be seven from apex downward, and similar seven, from down to vortex. **Life is a mysterious phenomenon, and mysterious are the ways to define or describe it.**

A stint of prosopopoeia in the scriptural prosody inevitably leads to some seeming inconsistency as also to an apparent derangement of its sequence which is partly because of the imagery of poetic diction of the seers and partly because of the apprehension lest the sublime theme should later be adulterated by the heterodox reasoning of the laity. **The cosmic science was considered to be the most secret and knowledge thereof was restricted to be imparted either to a disciple or to a friend[1] that is why the concealed moral in any description was not easy to paraphrase.**

The above extract from the *Vishnu Purana*[2] is no exception. The passage refers to *Sanandana* and the Mind Born sons of the progenitor-in-chief, named as *Brahma,* but this first progeny, being queerly without desire or passion though imbibed with holy wisdom, and undesirous of progeny, could not procreate. The anguished *Brahma,* therefore, begot another set of nine sons and nine daughters, and the first progeny in the name of *Sanandana* and others turned to be sterile, and in the interest of progeny, a union of the male and female of the specified nine sons was stipulated. The actual espousal pact impossible for ethereal entities, the postulate of marriage among them is imagery, meaning their cross-conjunction or trans-permutation. **This set of nine was a latent and transitional phase, incapable of reproducing a bisexual progeny; and this necessitated *Brahma* to issue forth another life named as *Rudra,* which was capable of producing a bisexual progeny, and *Brahma* commanded it to split into two separate bodies.**

Brahma is a term of art. *Brahma* and *Brahman* are both derived from root *Brih* which means large, great, and big

---

1. *Bhagwadgita,* 4/3; 9/1.
2. 1/7/3-15.

or beyond measure. The *n* in the letter term is an English suffix to distinguish the progenitor of life and the final absolute Reality. This simply means that the final or the first cause need not be confused with the creative cause of the universe. ***Brahman* is therefore, the first cause and *Brahma* is creative cause of life in the universe.**

According to the Upnishad,[1] the universe emerges from *Brahman,* sustained in *Brahman* and dissolves into the *Brahman.*

The above three are the modes of manifested and apparent things. They appear at a point of time, subsist for a given time and dissolve at a given point of time. These three modes are named in the scriptures as three different forces, responsible for creation, sustenance and dissolution. The scriptures named them artificially as *Brahma, Vishnu* and *Mahesh.*

In the aforesaid three incidents of creation, there is no concept of sex. They are simple life principles which have no consideration or relevance of being male or female. The principle itself has no sexual distinction, and **sex is therefore, a later stage of evolution.**

Sex is an outcome, of the stage where the monogenesis of life began bifurcating into the *X* and *Y* chromosomes. The *X* itself and the Y itself, are two monogenetic forces yet without discrimination of sex. The sex became an attribute of life only by accidental and disproportional conjunction or combination of the *X* and the *Y*. This disproportion in the conjunction of these two forces brought about the distinction and consciousness of being male and female.

The above episode of the *Vishnu Purana* testifies the fact that **the first life principle was without sex, the second hermaphrodite, the third the male and the**

---

1. *Chhandogya Upnishad,* 3/14/1.

female with their different organs, and the fourth race then became capable of sustaining the creative process through re-production. This way, creation was made simpler and easier.

Life in this way became multiplied on seed-to-seed basis and, unless their was a different seed, there could be no different product.

Nature at work without rest, continues to create newer and newer hermaphrodite forms or patterns as container of one or the other life principle, or the mould put by the life principle upon a particular form or pattern. **Nature being always at work there are different and different patterns created, sustained, destroyed or recreated, and the primary form or the pattern itself bifurcates itself into the male and female counterparts, by the oozing force of libido and reproduction thereafter follows as routine course.**

This logical and scientific account, displays the fallacies of modern evolutionary theories.

CHAPTER 4

FALLACIES OF MODERN EVOLUTIONARY THEORIES

SYNOPSIS

1. Species – Meaning and Implication
2. Life – Meaning of
3. Fundamental Agreement among Evolutionists
4. Theories Failing to Stand Metaphysical Tests
   4.1 Darwin's Theory
   4.2 Theory of Herbert Spencer
   4.3 Theory of Henry Bergson
   4.4 Insecure on Two Counts
5. Explanations in *Vedic* Law
   5.1 Standstill on Man
   5.2 Account of Procreation
   5.3 Origin of Female
6. Order of Origin of Species
7. Moot Question

1. Species – Meaning and Implication

According to Collins English Dictionary, a species is "a class of plants or animals whose members have the same main characteristics and are able to breed" with their counterpart.

In the Random House Dictionary of the English Language, the species are defined as "a class of individuals having same common characteristics or qualities, or as class of individuals of a distinct sort or kind."

In the biological sciences, the word 'species' denotes a major sub-division of a genus or sub-genus, regarded as basic category of biological classification, composed of related individuals which resemble one another.

The one distinguishing characteristic of any species is that they are able to breed among themselves but not able to breed with members of another species. In the cosmogenetic sense, the species are animate bodies, that is, life encased in a given physical outfit. Life emerges from the chrysalis of a cell. The assumption is twofold: first, that life does not evolve but emerges in a given set of conditions, and endures only in a carnal outfit, and, therefore, the rocks and boulders, though composed of the same material elements and having also a body of their own, have no life for lack of a carnal outfit; and, second, that the life pattern though blended with and embodied in its carnal lorica, is an independent entity, yet it is volatile, which has to dissipate, dissolve and wither away on the fatal event, known as the death.

All those who are born are doomed to die, says the *Bhagwadgita*[1]. All life must end in death. It is the doomed death associated with any life which distinguishes the species from other material objects. Death literally means the total and permanent cessation of all the vital functions of an animal or plant. The objects other than species may suffer change or become subject to decay or end by their total destruction but their extinction is entirely different from the destiny of death which all species have to inevitably meet, timely or untimely, be it an ant or a pachyderm; and no species can claim any fixed longevity and the age factor is totally irrelevant to the event of death; and the causes of death, too, may not be the same for any species or any member of the same species.

1. 2/27.

A most perspicuous fact as regards the animal species, is that from a cursory view of the structure and the peripheral extremities of an animal, a complete insight into the entire organism becomes perceptible. This extremity is the only clue to identifying a particular species, since this outlinear extremity remains the same even after death of the species. The skin and the flesh may decompose within given time after death, but the identity of the species persists through its skeleton. The plants are all the same biological species but have no skeleton and the logs of dry wood may not, without meticulous expertise, be distinguished as of one or the other tree. A plant lives so long as it stays green and is declared dead when it gets dry. The plant species have no heart and no blood to circulate in their corpus. The animal species, on the other hand, have a throbbing heart, and the moment of death and the cessation of the throb are inexceptionably conterminous.

Sex, fear and sleep, which are the essential attributes of animal life, are totally denied to plant life. Then again, plant species are all stationary and are totally immobile, and the motion in them is confined to the stirring of twigs, and leaves because of the impact and pressure of wind. In the body of any species, be it plant or animal, every element is so combined as to form a clear and distinct individuality. In the *homosapien*, the features of the face, the angularities of the skull, the height of the body, the length of the limbs, the bearing, the gait, the countenance, the sound, the gesture and traits of behavior, are all distinct and identifiable. This individuality among human beings is so pronounced that except in case of identical twins, each is different from the other in appearance, so much so that even the finger-prints of two individuals are not the same except in the rarest of rare cases. The animals, on the other hand, are endowed with a conspicuous similarity of behaviour, because it is purely instinctive. The cat would starve at the nicest fruit whereas the cow would instinctively refuse the most delicious of meat. The length or the size of an animal, in the same class, may differ in the hue and glow of their skins yet the most remarkable thing that the sound in a given class is audibly the same in any member of that class. The cuckoos coo, the snakes hiss, the cows bellow and the asses bray, indistinguishably in an equisonic voice.

However, the sounds of men differ even among members of same family or even among the sons or daughter of the same parents.

The evolutionary theories have missed to account for these rudimentary differences.

Apart from the plant and animal species, there have been innumerable avian and aquatic species, each subsuming thousands of its own sub-species. The butterfly park at Bangalore, India, claims to have identified as many as 30,000 varieties of this species; and it is difficult to classify this species either as a worm or a bird.

Then again, there seems to be no common thread in any respect, as regards the physiognomy or the behaviour pattern of these species and the basic difference between them fails to suggest any clue to the process of evolution of one into the other; and the fact that instead of their evolution from one into the other, they must have come into being at different stages of creation cannot be dismissed as incredible. Air being an evolute prior to water and, water being prior to earth, there is reason to believe that **avian species must have preceded the aquatic species, and the mammalia must have been the third race**, of course, preceded by the plant species.

The most innocuous inquisition is to reason out the myriadness not only of the species but also of their sub-species. Countless from the infinitesimal worm to the giant pachyderm, what chaos would have occurred if the world was infested only with one species all around, man or any other animal alone and exclusive, or if there were only males alone or females alone. The evolutionary theories have been found failing to explain even this toehold aspect.

The meaning of life may also be comprehended.

2. Life – Meaning of

The word 'life', in the Random House Dictionary of the English Language, has been devised to mean as under:

> "n. pl. lives, adj.-n. the condition that distinguishes animals and plants from inorganic objects and dead organisms, being manifested by growth through metabolism, reproduction and the power of adaptation to environment through changes originating internally.2. The sum of the distinguishing phenomena of plants and animals, esp. metabolism, growth, reproduction and adaptation to environment.3. The animate existence or term of animate existence of an individual; *to risk one's life.* 4. A corresponding state, existence or principle of existence conceived of as beginning to the soul. 5. The general or universal condition of human existence; *too bad but life is like that;* 6. any specified period of animate existence. 7. The term of existence, activity or effectiveness of something as a machine, lease, play, etc. 8. a living being; *several lives were lost.* 9. Living things collectively, whether animals or plants. 10. A particular aspect of existence. 11. The

> course of existence or sum of experiences and actions that constitute a person's existence......".

The word 'life', thus, connotes an animate existence and may also refer to the term, duration or longevity of such existence. The converse of life is death.

Breath is an essential attribute of existence; and since all living creatures inhale and exhale, life is identified with breath.

A creature is alive as long as it can breathe. The cessation of the activity of breath is surest test of an animal being dead.

Life is conditioned by hunger, and, of course, food is the salvo of life. Life, in any creature, sustains on the vitals of food and cannot subsist in absence thereof. Provision of food if suspended, the creature becomes exposed to death and must die, for want of food, within certain days depending upon the stoutness of his physique and stamina of its will. Abandonment of food foretells the approaching death of a creature; and since a creature may die of hunger, the *Upnishad*[1] has synonymised hunger with death. The same *Upanishad*[2] has classified consumable food into seven kinds, and though not specifically named, it is clarified that whatever is fit to be consumed, is a food. Myth or miracle, hunger has been recognised in psychology as the first inevitable instinct of a living creature, though it has not been possible for any science to exactly depict the form or the content of life as such.

For indeed, the animistic principle, whether conceived as breath, or anything as a spark, a light, heat, electricity, fluid or vibration, endows life and the destined withdrawal of which is made manifest by the state

1. *Brihadaranyak Upnishad,* 1/2/1-2.
2. 1/5/1.

known as death. Birth means the penetration of the cosmic life fluid trekking down in the deep channels of the surface of the body finally reaching the brain, and on death, returning to the ocean of the nature's vital fluid, respiring back from each cell as it had aspired them.

The species are, thus, frames of bodies endowed with life, but the moot point whether there is or ought to be an interrelation in or interdependence of life and the frame of body, whether any life can penetrate any frame or whether there is inevitable or immutable reciprocity between a given life and a given frame, can arouse no answer from any evolutionary theory so far propounded.

However, there is fundamental agreement on radical points among the evolutionists.

3. Fundamental Agreement among Evolutionists

A philosophy of evolution has to answer three fundamental questions:

(a) What evolves?

(b) How does it evolve?

(c) Why should it evolve?

Charles Darwin's work, *The Origin of Species by means of Natural Selection*, is an attempted answer to the first question, by stating that there is a common biological substance which evolves in a selective process in nature. The biological propensity to multiply more rapidly than nature can make allowance for life, compels certain species to perish even before they become capable to reproduce. Nature selects such of the species for survival as are found fittest in form to adapt to the conditions of the nature. The selective evolution of Darwin has two parts: the first maintaining a common substance or principle animating all forms of life; and the second, making the survival possible only of the fittest form of life.

The answer to the first question sums up the statement that what evolves is a single life principle with its inherent potentiality and the dynamicity to struggle for the best or the fittest form of life.

Answer to the second question comes form Herbert Spencer, primarily in his *First Principles* and elaborately in the *Principles of Biology.* The theory is that life is continuous adaptation of the biological or internal to the environmental or external relations. There is a reciprocal action between internal events. The life principle cannot maintain itself unless it succeeds in evolving a system of inner relations corresponding to external ones. The successive changes in the external world make impressions on the organism which also undergoes changes in consequence. The intimacy or intensity of correspondence between the inner and the outer relations results into higher and more developed forms of the organism. The intimacy of the correspondence invariably means the emergence of a new attribute in the organism, which is a new state of equilibrium maintained between the life principle and the environmental world.

This is emergent evolution, which propounds that the life principle requires, recognises and reconciles with an environmental reality in relation to which it exists and evolves; and that order and progress in life are always in relation with the environmental reality.

The third question is undertaken by Henry Bergson in his *Creative Evolution.* Bergson discovers the process of evolution in the clash and conflict of two opposite motions, that is:

(i) Life tending to go upward; and

(ii) Matter tending to fall downward

Life is one vital principle withstanding the resisting force of matter and struggling to break through the matter; and this breakthrough is possible on account of the creative force of life. Evolution is creative like the work of an artist. The creative impulse in life is an unpredictable deficiency of an unsatiated want. The vague and undefined impulse in the sightless organism leads him to struggle, enabling him, ultimately, in the creation of eyes, so that the instinct of perception is satisfied in the creation of the visual equipment which the organism had never premeditated prior to the creation of the apparatus for sight; and this affords one illustration out of the vast creative processes with which the organism is throughout engaged.

An epitomized version of the answer to the third question is a statement that the single life principle is instinctively compelled to evolve itself through a creative process in order to realize its nature and enjoy the consequences brought about by exploitation of its inner germane potentiality.

A denomination, suitably deserved by these three theories, can respectively, be recognised as the selective evolution attributable to Darwin, the emergent evolution, attributable to Spencer, and the creative evolution attributable to Bergson.

All the three theories are unanimous on the point that any evolutionary process would become explicable by reference to two principles: one, the boundless undifferentiated mass of animate life, namely, the life principle, a real consciousness heaped up in its purest or potential form; and the other, the boundless inert dynamicity of nature which is the principality of the matter. This dualism of the life and the nature, of vitality and dynamicity, the conscious dominating principle as the reservoir of energy or breakthrough *vis-à-vis* the dynamic but passive principle, is, in one of the

Upanishads,[1] denominated, respectively as *Pran* and *Rayi,* which are counterparts of the nomenclature of the *Purusha* and the *Prakriti,* roughly the sprit and the matter. On the interaction or partnership of these two, the *Samkhya* system of the Hindu philosophy has traced an elaborate theme of psycho-physical evolution.

Since from the point of view of the ultimate reality, there is no third principle, except sprit and matter, life can simply mean the sprit manifest in a mass of matter suitably evolved and developed by the integration of all the five species of matter, namely, the *aakash,* the air, the fire, the water and the earth, ready for penetration of the sprit therein. **Life is, thus, only the mundane dimension of the sprit.** Life is another name of matter animated by the sprit. The *Purusha* induced to penetrate the matter is *Pran* and the matter prepared to instil into it the sprit, is *Rayi;* and the two are cosmogenetic pseudonyms of the two metaphysical entities of the *Purusha* and the *Prakriti,* of the Samkhya philosophy; and there can be no other excogitation for the *Prashnopnishad* to coin the terms of *Pran* and *Rayi* respectively for *Purusha* and *Prakriti.*

This dualism is only a mode of monism, the monism of an infinite, impersonal, absolute reality. This infinite to Anaximander[2] is boundless mixture from which the things arise by separation. The infinite is an unseparated, undifferentiated mass. It is the same in Aristotle's *Metaphysics,* called as the indeterminate potential matter, indeterminate so long as it is potential and monistic, liable to become determinate in its descending into actual or pluralistic forms. It is this unqualitative stuff, without predicates and without attributes, that the *Rigveda*[3] has described as a **reality neither real nor unreal**. It is simply

1. The *prashnopnishad.*
2. *See* Burnet-Early Greek Philosophy, p. 59.
3. 10/129.

unmanifest which is impelled to become manifest by an indomitable impulse named as *Kama* or the subtle Eros, with its inner unction of a wanted or wanting satisfaction. The causality of this infinite stuff bifurcates itself and issues forth into a duality of the efficient or the dominant and the material or the subservient cause. Called by whatever name, life and nature, or energy and matter, or *Pran* and *Rayi*, or *Purusha* and *Prakriti*, they are respectively the maker, and the stuff for making. The *Brihadaranyak Upnished*[1] has described this process of bifurcation as compact division, just like the halves of a single cereal of grain, or corn, committed together in a compact attachment without any intervening space. The biological bifurcation of a unitary cell in the reproductive system and its subsequent fertilization in the genetic process explains this law.

The need of the infinite law was to become two and the initial two can be derived only by process of bifurcation of the existing unit. The separation or bifurcation of the infinite is the cosmic law of deriving two counterparts from one single entity. The process is the self-explained phenomenon where the bifurcated entities resist and oppose and interact upon or cooperate with each other. **This law is inevitably followed in the reproductive system where the cells multiply by bifurcation, reunion and re-bifurcation in a recurring order till it is closed up by a coat of skin. It is the bifurcation of one organism into two, and, then, the union of these two is required to produce a third. The attempt to propound a theory of evolution, without the first hand knowledge of the law of reproduction, would suffice in itself to reject the technique of all the three types of evolution, the selective by struggle, the**

1. 1/4.

emergent by adaptation and the creative by intuitive effort.

The one uniform life principle impregnating the one boundless unqualitative stuff, without predicates and bereft of attributes, has been described in the *Rigveda*[1] both as real and unreal, is unmanifest which is impelled to become manifest by an indomitable erotic impulse, known as the *Kama* which is the inner unction of the primordial reality to issue forth into creation. Short of this fundamental law of creation, the creative evolution in Bergson is only a fragmentary view, inconsistent with the creative impulse in nature. The unsatiated want for creation is incident of nature which creates things according to its preconceived patterns and the thing created has to rest content with its predestined apparatus because nature is free to issue forth into newer creations with more advanced or better, developed, types of apparatus.

Creation of species is recurrent impulse of nature and the wants of the creature are predetermined by the mould fixed on it by nature, and the creature can neither bargain nor betray what the nature has meant that organism to be. The wants and impulses of the creature are geared by the form it dons and the instincts instilled into it by nature. The creature cannot come into conflict with the order of nature but is impelled to comply with or carry out that innate order. **The creature has no choice of making additions to or diminutions from its given order.**

The physical frame of the creature is derived and developed in the environment following its own pattern set, and inculcated in its genes which throughout retain their content despite a change in the environment, and

1. 10/129.

the theory of adaptation to environment fails to harmonise itself with the genetic law inherent in the particular form of life.

A tree is bound to grow into the form betokened in its seed and the vagaries of the environment can affect only its physical growth or other deformities but not the intrinsic tendency of the seed which cannot create any thing other than its content, and the soil if unsuitable to the seed may probably destroy it altogether but if it allows the seed to grow, the seed has to carry out its own design and the soil cannot turn the wheat into barley or apple into orange.

The *survival of the fittest* argument is no logical appeal to the scheme of nature. **If the nature has chosen to endow particular species with particular sensitivity, or to deprive any species from any faculty, the soil cannot make up that deficiency, nor can it substitute one by another.** The faculty unique to any species, cannot be shared by any other species. All the three modern theories of evolution, therefore, fail to stand metaphysical tests.

4. Theories Failing to Stand Metaphysical Tests

4.1 Darwin's Theory

The evolution (or creation) of species is neither history nor psychology. As a biological phenomenon and as manifest principle of cosmic life, they are determined by metaphysical law.

Darwin and his adherents advocating the extinction of species on the clerihew of the survival of the fittest, would face a conundrum simply for their ignorance of how many different plants and animals there had been. Jeff Mc Neety, the chief scientist said[1] at the World Conservation Union, that some people who study insects

1. Reuters-report in the Hindustan Times, 20.03.2006.

think that there might be as many as 100 million species out here but taking a poll of biologists, most would say that there are somewhere around 15 million. There is no record, however, as to how many of them have or had become extinct, and when, why and how.

In the *Collin's English Dictionary,* a species is a class of plants or animals whose members have the same main characteristics and are able to breed with the other. The United Nations agreed in the year 2002 to reduce the rate at which animals and plants are disappearing. What has by now been known is that around 107 million plants and animal species have been identified and named by scientists.

There are probably few large mammals on land left to be discovered although a new deer and pig species were found in Vietnam in the 1990s in a region that had been heavily bombed by the United States during the war between the two centuries. Most of them have been named although new ones do crop up occasionally and a few extinct ones, such as the Ivory-Billed wood-pecker in the south of the United State, have reappeared, and there are many plants and insects and fish species that have been identified but not yet named. In South Africa, there are between 3000 to 4000 species, says John Leny, the co-author, with his wife, of a *Field Guide to Spiders,* in South Africa, and, as he says, unknown spiders would be lurking in gardens.

There is no scientific consensus on these issues, since scientists agree on the sobering fact that most of the species that walked, crawled or swam, or flew at some point of time, are now extinct despite their fitness.

The thesis that species fittest alone survive, or are allowed to survive, loses its ground from proved facts. In an era, say 18,00,00,000-13,00,00,000 years ago, known as the *Jurassic* age, the world was the habitat only of the dinosaurs in the zoological species and the conifers in the botanical species, and the **gigantic species of the dinosaurs, being the fittest and having no rival to combat them out, became extinct all abruptly and by one stroke of nature, nonchalant to their fitness for survival. In the present age, the tigers, the elephants and the camels, though fit qualitatively and quantitatively, and mighty also, are reported to be in a process of depletion.**

On the contrary, the weakest of the insects, the mosquitoes, the nudges, the reptiles and the pet species all exposed to numerous predators, are not reported to have depleted, their use or harm to other species being no question in the context.

That apart, there are several species having only a seasonal birth or growth or becoming extinct automatically at the end of their breeding session without the least relevance to their fitness or unfitness.

The lice in the hair, the insects in dung, and germs in a putrefied fruit, are born out of their own causes and die when removed from their base or exposed, with no reference to their fitness or otherwise.

Species on Earth are dying out faster than Darwin could imagine. A report released in the last week of March, 2006, at the United Nations Convention on Biological Diversity, in Curitiba, Brazil, stated that the declining number of plants, animals, insects and birds across the planet are adding up to the brink of extinction estimated to be one thousand times faster than in the past, and the catastrophe is counted as the sixth mass extermination since modern life began 650 million years ago and the worst since a comet snatched off the lights on the dinosaurs 65 million years ago.

It is again no wonder that some of the species held to be extinct elsewhere may by chance be searched out at any particular spot. For example, the long billed echidnas, a primitive egg-laying mammal, has been found to still exist in the mountains of the Indonesian province of West Papua.

Similarly, an underwater mountain off Sabia Island in the Caribbean, has come to knowledge of scientists as the habitat of more than a dozen new species of fish and sea weed.[1]

Forgetting how many species have disappeared, it is not precisely known how many species there still exist on the Earth. But, apart from freak of nature, the extinction of species can be attributed to several reasons other than Darwin's law of survival of the fittest.

This biological holocaust, that is, the wholesale extermination of one or the other species, may be cause for considerable apprehension to ecologists and the scientists alike, since it is possible in this age of wonders to make a Disneyland better than fabled in *Alice in Wonderland*, or to erect a Tajmahal, better than originally designed but it is impossible to replace a lost species. **Five million years is believed to be the maximum period for nature to regenerate a lost species.** Be that, as it may, the quest in hand is not extinction but origin of species; and origin would itself imply extinction, since **one who can make can also unmake; and this is all pragmatic law.**

The cause for extinction or depletion of species, include the loss of habitat not so much by climatic upsets as by human enterprises for development by expansion of agriculture and by deforestation warranted by needs of roads, hotels, rest houses and houses for inflating

1. Report in the Hindustan Times, New Delhi, 3.04.2006.

population, as also by poaching and overhunting of the wild life, coupled with depletion of nutrients from excessive use of chemical fertilizers, sewage, soil erosion and pollution of air and water, all these triggered by none else than the man in his craze for development.

Computation and struggle for existence is virtually not so stubborn among the brutes as among men. An animal hardly attacks another except in hunger or in self-defence. In his wanton zeal and envy in love and lust, for property or in professional rivalry, and in matters of social distinctions and political ambitions, human race stays and subsists in an overgrowth, despite the sordid odds of unabated ruse and rancours, whereas the animals even in absence of sins and sorrows surrounding them, are vulnerable to extinction, thus, leaving in lurch the law of survival of the fittest, or, in other words, the struggle for existence. **Nature aspires, rather conspires, to preserve man as the supreme life for reasons other than those surmised by Darwin.**

The credulous aspect but otherwise the weakest plank in the Darwinian theory, is to trace the origin of man from the ape without explanation of the numerous distinctions in the ape species itself. There being no explanation of the descent of the ape itself among the brands of the chimp, the *guerilla* or the *baboon*, and no plausible link traceable for reasoning out the surfeiting breeds among the simian breed, it would be making but a bewildered incertitude first to arrogate one as being evolved of the other as well as to fix descent of man to any particular simian.

Because of the failure to explain whether the different varieties among the ape species, is aleatory or evolutionary, the surmise of decent of man from ape is a figment.

There have been several mammals in the feline species but taking the mighty tiger and the nimble cat, the Darwinian theory cannot explain whether the cat has evolved into a tiger or the tiger has devolved into the cat. This creates serious dent in the Darwinian Theory. The case of donkeys, mules and horses is not different from zebras in ocular skeletal identity, and there is no clue which of them stands evolved from what. The snakes, vipers and pythons, visible in hundreds of the reptile destiny despite their biological affinity, do not provide any evolutionary link among them.

Lessons in human anatomy are imparted by dissections of a frog and not an ape when the anatomy of ape would have matched with that of the human in more approximate degrees.

All these objections have not been explained in the Darwinian Theory.

The deceptive resemblance between a cock and a peacock may confuse a child to explain the inherent difference between the two but the ocular dissimilarity between a peacock and a peahen is still astounding where the prettiness of the female is far less attractive than that of its male counterpart.

The skeletal identity between the lizard and the dinosaur is an enigma. It is difficult to infer whether the lizard is a reduced form of the dinosaur or the dinosaur is an enlarged edition of the lizard. There is otherwise no evidence whether the lizard or the dinosaur came first.

Biological scientists and paleontologists, and others, are at times undertaking an expedition into the inhospitable icy deserts and elsewhere in search of the fossils and their findings of having come across some new species of plants or animals, may be adventitious discovery but without clue to what process of evolution such species have come about.

Parts of the world, then, represent to be the exclusive habitat for certain species, for example, the giraffe or an antelope having an ox-like head in Africa, and the kangaroo with its marsupial sack, in Australia and adjacent Islands but absent in other parts, may conceivably trace their genesis to peculiar climatic or topographical considerations than to any evolutionary process.

Lastly, the principles propounded by Darwin are not at all applicable, nor has he bothered to apply them, to the botanical species.

If the original species can be made explicable with reference to two principles, one the boundless undifferentiated mass of animate life, namely, the life principle, that is a real spirit or consciousness mustered in its purest or potential forms, and, the other, the boundless inert dynamicity of nature, that is, the principality of the matter, regarded to in the *Prashnopnishad* as the *Pran* and the *Rayi*, then, the same principle must equally apply to the origin of all species in the biological domain whether on the botanical or the zoological side.

Those engaged in the study of fossils are not farther from Darwin since their findings are directed to provide a moonshine of the evidence of an animal that was on the verge of its transition from the water to the land. All their endeavor proceeds on a smug belief that they would succeed to capture the missing link between the fish and the land animals, demarcating how the creatures first walked out of the water on and upto the dry land, conceivably more than 375 millions of years ago though bereft of their concern to explain the choice of nature in providing hundreds of varieties of the shark and the whale, being each a species in its own, always begetting their like instead of evolving into anything different. The reptiles and ants, in their multiplex varieties, have not been scientifically proved to be prone to the art of cross-breeding, and are begetting their own like, with no tendency to evolve into anything different.

Extinction of species to Darwin was part of evolutionary game. The modern environmentalists and ecologists cogitate on this problem rather on utilitarian propositions.

It is believed, though without any cogent scientific data, that each creature in the universe has its own utility. It is propounded that each organism has its own role in upholding the environmental balance and in interlinking the creaturehood into the vast continuous chain of life, and the damage done to any is danger to the environmental balance. Jainism and Buddhism have, therefore, advocated non-violence as the ideal cult.

Nonviolence as the prime cult is vigorously preached in the *Shantiprava* of the *Mahabharata*, by *Yudhishthir*; the *Pandava* King; The characteristic of the real erudite, in the *Bhagwadgita*,[1] is the practice of looking with the same eye on a *Brahmin* endowed with learning and culture, a cow, an elephant, a dog and a pariah too. All that, is on the settled belief that the cosmic spirit is one and the same in any creature, from the tiniest of ant to the gigantic pachyderm, and apart from this spiritual tenet as part of the cosmic ethos, **there is no reference in the *Vedic* texts to any principle like environmental balance, merely because of preservation of the species, all or some of them in particular.**

The *Atharva Veda*[2] has condemned oblation of limbs of cattle in fire. The renowned pathological treatise of *Charaka*, in the chapter on animal sacrifice, states that

1. 5/18.
2. 7/5/5.

cattle are meant to adorn the rituals but not for killing. The *Mahabharata*[1] abhors killing of cattle in sacrificial rituals which is reiterated in the *Samkhya Sutra* of *Kanad*, by retorting that if heaven is gained by killing the cattle, what and for whom the hell is meant for.

In the *Padma Purana*[2], those who sacrifice animals, it is said, are doomed to perdition, and the *Rigveda*[3] ordains that no one shall flail the cow, the sheep or the goat, nor any biped. In the *Atharva Veda*[4], the livestock is described as the sixth among life made manifest by the creator. Cruelty to animals is condemned in the *Manusmriti*[5] by homilies that the killer of cattle is doomed to die as many times as there are hair on the skin of the cattle, and that even after death, he shall have no peace.

All these are moral adjurations and the environmental problems of the present day have induced the modern thought to arrogate an environmental consciousness even to the *Vedic* age.

In the *Vedic* age, environmental faith had its anchorage only in the practice of the *Yajna*, that is, the ceremonial customary sacrificial fire and a duty was enjoined on every household to perform it.

The *Bhagwadgita*[6] states:

> "Having created mankind along with the spirit of sacrifice, at the beginning of creation, the Creator, the Lord of creatures, said to them: 'you shall prosper by this; may this yield the happiness you seek.'

1. *Shantiprava*, Ch.-226.
2. 104/5.
3. 1/46.
4. 15/15.
5. 5/38,45.
6. 3/10-12.

> "Foster the gods through sacrifice, and let the gods be gracious to you. Each fostering the other disinterestedly, you will attain highest good.
>
> "Fostered by sacrifice, the gods will surely bestow on you without even asking for that, all the desired happiness; but he who enjoys the gifts bestowed by them, without giving them in return by the *Yajna*, is an affirmed thief."

The philosophy of spiritual identity in the entire creaturehood is warm with a moral tone of cosmic justice that all creatures equally partaking the cosmic spirit are equal partners in the chain of cosmic creation and have to be treated alike, since the quality of spirit does not derogate merely by dwelling in a lower creature. But, this spiritual identity cannot be confounded with the so-called environmental balance.

However, the conceptions of the environmentalists are curious and chimerical.

Several of the animal and the bird species destroy the obnoxious insects and help growth of vegetation through spreading and scattering the seeds they feast upon. The birds and animals, to considerable extent, do also cause damage to the crops, but that is as the environmentalists would say, because of depredation of forest tracts. Barring the onslaught of man on forests and their inmates, the natural balance in environment would take its own course thereby liquidating the damage which may be trivial in comparison to their usefulness, subscribed, if any, by these creatures to the fruits or cereals.

It is again no strong logic for preservation of the animal species that they are the first subject of scientific or medical experiments, as for example, a bitch was selected to be the first creature to travel into the cosmic space, or thousands of frogs are needed for lessons in the medical science, or that rats or apes are utilized in ascertaining the after-effects of new medicinal inventions, and so on, yet the fact remains, and which is of utmost anxiety to the environmentalists, that unless the devastation of these and other species merely for profit or sport is brought to an end, the rarest of the rare species and sub-species of the lower order will become extinct so that there would be men and men all around the earth with the inherent danger of their own existence because of environmental imbalance.

There is one commendable aspect of Darwin's theory that he has attributed the extinction of species to the choice of nature, the fallacy in his survival of the fittest principle notwithstanding, but the environmentalists have failed to reason out what havoc would have been if one or the other species would or should have become extinct from the planet. **The species become extinct by frenzy of nature to withdraw one or the other pattern of life from its scheme of creation.**

The earth suffered no cataclysm when by one catastrophic impulse of nature, the whole race of dinosaurs, both carnivorous and herbivorous, which once thronged and overcharged the earth, sank into annihilation. The nature in due course substituted that extinct race by some new or newer race or races.

If life on earth is impossible without intervention of nature, there is no reason to surmise that life can become extinct merely by the misdeeds of men. **If nature continues to produce some species, no human endeavour can cause its extinction.**

Origin of species by natural selection may be all right, provided this selection is attributed to nature itself, whether at random or by way of some prodigious experiments, for one reason or other or for none, and for reason or for no reason, the nature has not stopped creation of species, newer and newer, including the weakest, shortlived, or with negligible longevity, or the unfit type, and in the scheme of nature, there may be scope for trial and error, for betterment or improvement, but fitness or utility of particular species fails to fit in with any logical relevance.

The environmentalists may be right in saying that each creature on earth has its utility yet it is for man to associate particular utility with particular creature. **The laws of nature are rational having no relevance to utility. Nature has never meant snakes to be killed or fish to be eaten, nor an ox to work on fields and the horse on roads.** Man's onslaught on his environment is like self-inflicted wound, without damaging the innate texture of nature, though acting contrary to nature may have unnatural consequences.

Predicating the extinction of one or the other species to cosmic imbalance is itself an imbalanced thought.

The origin of earth is calculated on surmises to be same time between 450,000,0000 to 600,000,0000 years ago, and the point of time for the origin of life on earth may yet be a pretended imagery, and **if there was no cosmic imbalance without any species on earth, it is ideationally incorrect to conceive the extinction of some species responsible for cosmic imbalance** when there is no dearth of knowledge that new species have taken place with or without any regard to extinction of any, and newer and newer may yet be in the offing in the manufactory of nature.

As back as about 500 B.C. Anaximander, the Greek philosopher of the Milesian School, had propounded that each cosmic element is perpetually attempting to enlarge its empire but there is a kind of necessity or natural law which perpetually redresses the balance. There is an innate potentiality in nature to control its own aberrations and keep its intrinsic balance.

The nature generates this hostility by itself and brings about a truce again by itself. The inherent prepotency of nature to recuperate its balance is complete answer to the anxiety of the environmentalists about extinction or depletion of any species. As for Darwin's theory, nature sets particular conditions for particular species to generate, and given the specific conditions, the imprints set by cosmic skill descend unto those conditions to generate and survive so long as the conditions suitable for their survival endure; and the nature's manufactory, as the *Rigveda*[1] says, is occupied with the anxiety of moulding newer and newer patterns just as a blacksmith moulds his wares by working at his bellows. **The earth only breeds and nurtures the specimens ingested into it by that manufactory, but the nature is master of its speciology.**

This capacity of nature to resume and restore its balance is represented in the *Vedic* philosophy by the principle of *Rta* which composes the strife between the good and the evil, and it is the same thing depicted allegorically as the war between the gods and the demons, which are only the two opposites pervading the real content of nature.

Not unlike Darwin, the theory of emergent evolution propounded by Herbert Spencer is not without its logical infirmities.

4.2 *Theory of Herbert Spencer*

The double conclusions of scientists, one that the species lose their last vestigiaries if the climatic change is

1. 10/72.

allowed to continue unchecked, which means that the climatic change is rapidly becoming the most serious threat to the planet's bio-diversity which proposition, comes from T. Malcom, the Assistant Professor of Forestry at the university of Toronto, and, the second, that it is not a sure thing that Ardipithecus had evolved into Australopithecus, because both are two different species with the major noticeable difference between the two being that the latter is endowed with bigger chewing teeth suited to eating harder food, and this proposition has come from Berhane, an Ethiopian Anthropologist.

Both these findings had been released in Washington on April 13, 2006 in the Journal *Nature*.

The climatic conditions and the environment being typically and characteristically the same, Australopithecus had bigger teeth in comparison to the Ardipithecus. In the absence of bigger teeth, the latter could thrive only on softer wood. Both survived in one and the same habitat and there were both the harder and the softer food, available on the same land.

This is because there is different preference for food in different species, chosen by each in accordance with what suited them out of habit or rapacity or spontaneity. Even among man, placed in similar conditions, they would differ in matters of cuisine and accoutrement, with the only consideration that whereas men choose mostly by taste and temperament, animals do it by instinct. The deer and the lion, are inmates of the same habitat, yet the former would starve on the most staple of flesh whereas the latter would reject the most delicious of the fruit. Camels and goats are both domestic pets accustomed to the same atmosphere, and both have common relish for leaves of margosa tree, yet the latter would take only when served whereas the former would stretch his neck and pluck his morsel direct from the twig; and the assumption, on the line of Spencer's theory, would be perceptibly fantastic that the neck of the camel has gradually evolved to its present length in order only to reach the twigs when the camel, too, has a variety of taste other than the margosa leaves. The cat and the tiger though biologically of the same phylum, yet the former is both vegetarian and non-vegetarian whereas the latter is bound, by nature to be carnivores; and, curiously enough, the non-vegetarian taste of the cat is confined to the flesh of rats or birds. The dinosaur again, illustrates the carnivorous and the herbivorous taste in two different classes of the same species.

Spencer would suggest that the imprint of stripes on the hides of certain species was attributable to the rays of Sun filtering through the greenery of trees in dense forests. The theory is fallacious right from its inceptions. Dense forest is condition precedent to any wild life, which expression denotes a non-domestic animal, ferocious or gentle, yet the stripe on skin is peculiar only to the tiger or the zebra but the lion has no stripes despite the fact that it is as ferocious as tiger and residing in the same habitat. The deer and the antelope may have other spots or speckles on their skin yet not the same as that of the tiger. The monopoly of the tiger on the stripes, peculiar to it, can hardly have any explanation in Spencer's theory. The nigrescent kept even in Iceland are liable to breed exactly their like and the Europeans based in India continue to bear the same complexion as their ancestors. **The whites are the same white even after their immigration in the tropical countries.** Even assuming that the immigrants from one to another climate are prone to characteristically show a slight change in their complexion, the change becomes at once attributable to the effect of the particular climate, and the theory of adaptation to the environment is reversed into the theory of effect of climate on the species. **The species do not adapt to the environment but the environment affects the species.** If the stripes on tiger are because of the filtering of the Sun through the green leaves, the tiger has no choice of its own but is only the recipient of or rather servient to, the peculiar climatic effects.

The reason that the species develop certain peculiar and apparent characteristics in their bodies as an aid to concealing their presence from the predator, is, again, unsustainable because it provides the same opportunity to the predators to conceal from their perdu and hide their presence from their prey. The assumption that creatures are prone to exhibit specific chromatic characteristics by force of their ambience, would, on other hand, testify that whereas the nature is active, the creatures have only a passive role in the environment to which they are exposed.

Analysed strictly, the adaptation to environment theory is more a psychological than a physiological phenomenon. The animals tamed and trained in sports adapt to the discipline of their trainer and succeed in giving performances unusual and unexpected, which is the same thing as a convict adapting to the discipline of the jail authority. Finally, the multichromatic tress or plumes of cock can be explained neither by heredity nor by environment since the chicken may not inherit the colour of their parents in their feathers, nor can it be ascribed to any environmental effect as similarly as the calves may not have the same hue on their skins as that of their parents. The mystery is insoluble and reason is compelled to rely for that on freak or frenzy of nature. **No logic can explain the origin and the mysteries of the cosmos.** The environment can have its own effect without anticipating adaptation.

The theory of creative evolution of Bergson is, without any evidence.

4.3 *Theory of Bergson*

The fundamental fallacy of creative evolution is its belief that matter tends to fall downward and life tends to go upward.

Life and matter do constitute an integrated whole. It is life, that is, the tendency of life to become manifest in finite species which makes the matter to fall downward. What tends to or ought to tend upward is the entity, triumvirately known in *Vedic* philosophy as the spirit, soul or the *Atman*. The paradox is that the tree of life is supine having its root upward and trunk downward[1] and it is through a cosmic exercise that the spirit is made to go upward for its final dissociation from life, and it is upto this end that the evolution comes to its vortex on the advent on earth of the human being.

The evolutionists have no answer to the standstill of the evolution, or its process, after advent of the man. **The cosmic urge was creation of the best and the perfect and the most veritable and versatile life whereafter the cosmic exhortation required man to elevate himself spiritually** as the *Chhandogya* and the *Brihadaranyak Upanishads* have set forth in their homilies. The moral of *Upnishad* is to explain life in spiritual terms. Spiritual elevation is the highest aim of life and the human life must make efforts that chances of rebirth are nullified.

Life is not a process explained by complacence of the evolutionists. It is a self-ordered process bound by its own laws which cannot be transgressed.

The organs in the organism are not because of the supposed unrest for an unfulfilled want but verily because of the cosmic urge for spiritual elevation.

1. *Bhagwadgita,* 15/1; *Kathopnishad,* 2/3/1.

Man is a miniature cosmos. The human physiognomy is micro-assemblement of the substances and forces of nature. The substances and forces conceived as operative in the cosmos are meticulously concentrated in the human body in a design corresponding to the cosmic phenomenon. It is the man alone who has all the vital forces of nature located on particular seats in his body.

Man being a model of the creative art of nature, is not imperfect in any sense. It is fully accomplished and well equipped, and no unsatiated want or urge can be imputed to it. The only urge is to become spiritually one with the cosmic soul.

The configuration of creatures and the breakthrough of their sense organs is not a blind urge within the creature but is process of cosmic exertion. This miraculous exertion is conceived in the *Upnishad*[1] as the *Tapah* which literally means ascetic toil, representing the activity of incubation of the egg or the embryo. It is this incubated heat which makes the egg erupt, just as the atmospheric calefaction aided by the inner moisture of the plant forces the bud to bloom into a flower. Just as the outer shell of an egg serves as a cover of the inner content of its yolk, the embryo is covered by its amnionic sack. What the hen does on the egg from outside, the mother does it inside her womb and, at a given degree of incubation, the amnion rips apart in the same way as the eruption of the egg.

The above *Upnishad* describes the first incidence of eruption in the sap of the orifice of mouth to become an organ for the intake of food; and the elemental fire inside the mouth at once gushes out in the form of voice or speech; and this explains the first cry of the baby on birth. Nostrils were thereafter formed by the outburst of

1. *Aitereya Upnishad,* 1/4.

the elemental air, which became the life breath of the new born. In the mouth then emerged the tongue which served both as medium of speech and taste answering to the elemental water. The incubated heat then re-exerted to form the two cavities for the eyes to emerge, representing the element of Sun. The process followed thereafter to form the auditory holes representing the element of *aakash* or space and served as receptacles of sound.

Finally, the skin developed as an outer coat of the creature, and tresses of hair came to cover the skull and the bristles emerged out of the skin. The energy of Moon rested in the mind. Thereafter, the navel was formed which regulated the flatus and then the anus for excretion, and, eventually, the phallus for emission of semen and for micturition. This is a full, correct and phased account of the constitution of the body of a creature, where everything occurs according to the design and there is nothing like an unfulfilled want or unsatiated desire.

The breakthrough of the organs, motor or sensory, is plan of nature to manifest all or any of its faculties in the creature; and nothing can come merely by inner unction. **All that comes about is by nature's will and nothing can be brought about unless it was inherent in nature.** The *Bhagwadgita*[1] preaches that all events are performed by the modes of nature and it is delusion to hold that some creature had done it by the power of its will.

The origin of life is a singular, continuous uniform process though the components of creation share it on gradually ascending orders. The nature is busy with its function in shuffling and reshuffling of these components of creation to bring about innumerable patterns of life.

1. 3/27.

The creatures of higher as well as of the lower order, all, issue forth from the ovary of the nature, though it is not out of place to assume that in the animal world, the nature proceeded to create the most efficient and fully equipped creatures in an ascending order after creating the less equipped or imperfect ones otherwise lacking any accessory of life. **It is not against logical acceptability that the more equipped in form or in ability, could or should have come after the less equipped or the deficient ones.**

The *Upnishad*[1], narrates how the cosmic energy had devised to improve the succeeding forms of life, after the preceding ones. The *Upnishad* conceived that the nature having endowed the organism with all the attributes, the organism felt tormented by hunger and thirst, and craved for the fittest form of body for satiating its instinctive demands. The cosmic agency of creation initially designed the form of a cow which was not found appropriate because the same was not functionally perfect. Next, then, was presented an equine figure, which, too, was found to be imperfect in several aspects. Finally, then, came the human form, and, there being nothing better in conception, the experiment ended and the human figure, thus, stayed as the perfect model.

The process epitomized above is illustrative and not exhaustive; nor could it be in the esoteric way of description peculiar to any scripture. The moral lies only in distinguishing the perfect from the imperfect, or, stated differently, the cosmic meticulousness in heaven brought about a flawless exquisite abode for the life, yet without discriminating the essence or sanctity of life despite the imperfection or deficiency of the frame in which it gets encased. In the cosmic ethos and in the piety for life, the

1. *Aitereya Upnishad,* 1/2/2.

physical frames are not relevant. It is the same spirit which pervades all species which, as the *Bhagwadgita*[1] says, share the same stream of life, be it the erudite scholar, the pariah or the cow, the bitch or the elephant. The enumeration, here, again, is illustrative and discerning without being exhaustive.

The physical frame of a creature is an integrated and solidified compound of the five elements of nature, the *aakash*, air, fire, water and earth, which have each an attribute respectively of sound, touch, sight, taste and smell. These components when present in the organism, the five sense organs are most likely to develop and emerge at their appropriate places in the animate creature except either when there is some inherent genetic defect liable to impair any such apparatus in the body, or when the nature has itself decided to keep any creature without any such apparatus or instrument.

The second alternative has been recently evidenced by the sudden discovery of a deep underground cavern in Israel, explored by a youth. The cavern, since named as Iyolon, is an impassable crust of earth beneath thick layers of choke and has also a lake therein, covering two and half kilometers. It is stated[2] that the cavern represents a complete eco-system. The cavern is the abode of eight completely new species. The scientists of the Hebrew University, Jerusalem, have affirmed the presence in this eco-system of a avian species and an albino and a new species of scorpions. Several new species are likely to be identified in this eco-system but the thing of real significance in this context is that the species in existence in this cavern are all blind, though the origin of all such species has been traced to 50,00,000

1. 5/18.
2. A report in the monthly magazine, *Kadambini*, New Delhi, January, 2007.

years back. The cavern is wrapped up in total darkness and the source of energy in this cavern is yet unknown when, obviously, the green vegetational energy is not only absent but totally impossible in the existing conditions of that cavern.

The evolutionists are, again, insecure on two counts.

4.4 Insecure on Two Counts

The classical evolutionists have failed, firstly to account for the standstill of the evolutionary process right at the advent of man and, second, that they have not been able to account for the origin of the female.

The *Vedic* law has adequate explanations on both these points.

5. Explanations in *Vedic* Law

5.1 Standstill on Man

Life, as all agree, is a singular, uniform continuous phenomenon, where the components of creation share it on gradually ascending orders providing due margin for competition among the preceding orders.

The first part of this proposition is accurate but the second, erroneous.

The one single continuous process can never allow competition. Competition occurs where processes are manifold. Competition is not natural but artificial where several beings similarly situated strive for a common goal. The lion is carnivorous but the cow is herbivorous, but it is no ground to hold that there is competition between the two species. Different behaviors and different addictions are alien to the concept of competition. Competition can exist among the species of one given order but where the orders are themselves different, it is absurd to infer any competition. One order may be a friend or foe of the other, but competition has no role to play in matters of necessities or intrinsic differences.

In the creative process of nature, life issues forth from cosmic energy in the form of patterns or archetypes; and in that process each type or pattern is coincident and the orders as a whole may approbate a purview of existence in a common scheme of co-partnership which is wholly averse to ignoble competition; and the inherent idiosyncrasy peculiar to one order of life cannot be misnamed arbitrarily as competition.

The recondite enigma of nature is psycho-physical parallelism. The reality is not one but two-in-one, that is, spirit and matter, described in the *Rigveda*[1] as both real and unreal. Had it been one alone, there could have been no evolution. The instinct of the one to become many cannot be materialized without being two. **The one cannot be multiplied by itself.** It is the multiplication and permutation of two that leads to many. The unmanifest spirit works only through the manifest matter. The spirit rests into the matter with a view to realising itself, and the too many frames of body are its experiments in what frame it could realise itself best.

The cosmic life, therefore, manifests itself into patterns or archetypes whereof each is a carrier both of a dynamic life and an active spirit, and the impenetrable plan of nature is the exertion of one and the same spirit in different orders of life with purpose to discern what pattern of life can succour its endeavour for the highest spiritual attainment. Spiritual realisation is experience, through which the sentient spirit becomes conscious of its potentiality; and, since there can be no experience without the accessories of sense organs, the nature endows each life with different capacity of sensation through different limitations of mind with an urge to get at the most exquisite frame probablising the senses to become the most furnished and the most equipped.

1. 10/129.

The difference in biological dexterity, involving the formation, adjustment and juxtaposition of the motor organs or, in psychological capacity, involving the endowment, functional strength and control of sense organs among the classes of crated beings, has been with a view to upgrading of the spirit on gradually higher planes. **Each lower order is an incentive for onward progression which marks the continuity of the stream of life in the escalation of spiritual exhilaration.** Whereas the brute would devour the eatables only to satiate his hunger, the human being relishes his food in a variety of ways involving combinations or modifications. These sophistications, added to the instinctive taste, is spirituality. **Emotional satisfaction is spiritual necessity.**

The brute associates with his female counterpart just for mating. The human being enjoys it also for his spiritual contentment, and, even for that crude act, has compiled a complete science.

It is not unlikely that there have been all sorts of experiments on these two fundamentally crude instincts of hunger and sex. These experiments are evidence of the degree of spiritual relish these two instincts can create. **All tastes, taboos and totems, and even addictions, are spiritually relished.** Such spiritual experience is most endowed on man. The man stands at the apex of creaturehood, because he can meditate on things on which the lower brutes cannot concentrate. The spiritual realisation is maximum in man. It is man alone and not other animals, who can attain his *Summum Bonum*.

The supposed natural selection is a gradual progression of the simple compounds of elements of nature into the stream of organic composition. The memoirs of chemical evolution remind of the strides taken by life for its emergence from the earliest appetitive stage into the ultimate meditative state. The spirit being the same in any creature, it is compressed in the brute but evolved to its exuberance in man.

A brute works by mere motivations. On the other hand, man can deliberate and decide by meditation, and this power to meditate vouches the fullest development of the spirit. The aim of evolution has been to reach the highest stage of meditation which the nature's exertion could attain only in man, standing, therefore, at apex of the process. The endowment of spirit in a lower or upper grade, is nature's experiment in its alchemy; and a creature becomes endowed with a spirit the moment the solar energy penetrates into the physical frame of the creature, and the creature is animated thereby.

The origin of life, is, thus, traced to the alchemy of lighter compounds diffused freely in nature in the substantive forms of carbon, hydrogen, oxygen and nitrogen, combining with each other and resulting into the formation of the basic compounds of water, ammonia and methane.

The transformation of these simple compounds, in their turn, resulted into the formation of other sophisticated compounds, like glucose, glycerin and the fatty acids; and the process continued until the creation of virus, considered to be the first representative of embodied life.

Composed only of nucleic acid, the virus reacted upon another compound of protein, and a combination of the two succeeded in bringing about the origin of the nucleo-protein endowed with the faculty of reproduction. The first step towards emergence of the spirit was the origin of appetitive life, capable of nothing more than the appetite of reproduction.

The fermentation of life had soon to discover that even the crude appetence could not be prolonged without the ingestion of energy. The primal life, arrested in the chrysalis of a single cell, aspired to come into contact with the cosmic source of energy. The Sun being the single source of energy, cellular life came in communion with the Sun. The Sun is nucleus of the universe, and since a communion could be possible only from nucleus to nucleus, the cellular life, so far, without a nucleus had to develop a nucleus for generation into it of a substance known as the chlorophyll meant as an absorbent of solar energy, with the advantage of the appetitive life evolving into the vegetative life. Vegetation being the primary food to sustain animate life, the vegetation became susceptible to evolve into the animal life, which is not yet meditative life. The nature aspired yet to evolve into a spiritual or meditative life.

The Sun as the centre of the universe, becomes automatically the sustainer of life. This affords sufficient evidence of the fact that the sustenance of life is a singular, uniform and continuous phenomenon making it possible for the components or creation to share the universal spirit on unlike but gradually ascending orders. In this ascending order of creation, the vegetative life, thus, automatically evolved into the animal life or the instinctive life; and the next ascending order of life finally culminated into the meditative life of man. **Vegetative life is beginning and the meditative life is the goal.**

The advent of man, thus, marked the ultimate evolution of life and the highest order of spirit in man served as an aid to the fullest evolution of life. And this explains the standstill of evolutionary process on the event of advent of man where the evolution of life became instrumental to evaluation of life.

Having brought life to its aspired meditative stage, the biological evolution culminated its purpose, leaving the lower order undisturbed, as they were, with their power of reproduction and their liberty to multiply without any endeavour of resurrection of those which had become extinct, since the nature yet remained in its full prolific swing, to create newer and newer species. The skill of nature having realised its summit, in the evolution of the meditative life in man, there was no urge for creation of species higher than man, though it never hesitated to produce on earth rare, super-powered creatures when the times so demanded, as affirmed in the *Bhagwadgita*[1] that whenever righteousness is on decline and unrighteousness is gaining ground, the nature embodies itself into rare virtuous super souls with the aim of protection of values and sacred aims of life; and for extirpation of the evil doer as also for establishing righteousness on a firm footing, and the birth of such super souls as *Rama, Krishna, Buddha, Jesus,* and the like, stands in ample evidence of that assertion, and history knows the purpose for which these virile and virtuous souls appeared on earth.

The evolutionary process from the lowest appetitive life to the highest meditative life has aptly been demonstrated in the *Chhandogya Upnishad.*[2] The esoteric statement is:

> "the earth is the sap of all beings; the sap of earth is water; the sap of water is vegetation; the sap of vegetation is the person; the sap of the person is his consciousness; the sap of consciousness is intellect; the sap of intellect is spirit; and the sap of spirit is the plenum of the person."

1. 4/7-8.
2. 1/1/2.

The term 'sap' literally means honey, something sweet, or delightful. The word 'sap' connotes an essence, juice or gravy. The word 'sap' can also represent the basal substance responsible for the causation of a thing; and the substance is the material cause of that thing. The thing made out of the form given to the substance is a process which sustains the substance but gives it a typical shape, in the same way as a goldsmith moulds different ornaments or the pot-smith moulds different models of clay. The substance being the same, its configurations can be multiplex. The mould when contemplated to be executed was a cause but when transformed into matter, it stayed as effect. The substance serves both as its cause and effect.

The *Samskrit* term for sap is *Madhu* which, in the context, means the essence of life, and the above statement in the *Upnishad* explains and enumerates the chain or the causal process of evolution of life from the appetitive to its meditative stage. The statement starts from the earth. The earth is essence of all beings. The earth is the cause of all things, and all beings are born of the earth, and the earth is adored as mother, because it is maternal or material cause of all animate beings. The earth is the last of the five elements and water is the immediate predecessor of the earth. Hence, water is essence of earth. Vegetation can sprout and grow with the help of water. Water is essence of vegetation. Fruits and cereals are produced from water, and water is sap of anything edible as food. This food is essence of life.

The *Bhagwadgita*[1] and the *Manusmriti*[2] agree on the causal chain reiterating that the animate creatures are born from cereal, the cereal is born from water, and

1. 3/14.
2. 3/76.

water is born of *Yajna*. The word *Yajna* denotes the cosmic chain of causation. The creative activity is literally equivalent to a continuous *Yajna*, which is an inter-play of the cosmic fire in five consecutive rounds, named as the *Panchagni Vidya*[1] or the science of five fires. The cosmic creative process is a *Yajna* in the sense that, it is a processing of the cosmic fires into five consecutive stages. It is in the fifth round that, the cosmic spark of life becomes personified into a given frame.

The last round of fire is the processing of the digested food into the semen and when the semen is deposited in the womb of a woman, a person is born. Since the creative activity is an activity bought about by operations of fire, it is named as *Yajna*. **The word *Yajna* is synonym of fire.** The *Vedic* word for 'person' is '*Purusha*'.

The digestive process initially transforms the nutrients of food into sappy fluids and by a number of further chemical processes, the derived fluid is formed into blood, which in the final process, gets deposited in the seminal vesicle of the body and when discharged on consummation of coitus gets into the ovary of the female counterpart to impregnate her and to make her give birth to a creature in full form.

The *Chhandogya Upnishad*[2] has simply condensed this exoteric truth in a prosodic way, and explains the next phase of endowment of a particular personality on the creature so born.

The attribute of a personality is common to all creatures. The term 'personality' need not, hence, the confused as the characteristic personage of the human being. **Personality is an abstract term, denoting the quality of being in an organised mass of body and**

1. *See* Heading 3.4 in Ch.-III.
2. 1/1/2.

the consciousness. The word *'Purusha'* in *Samskrit* is equivalent for 'person' and is a definitive term.

Shankaracharya in his commentary on the *Bhagwadgita*[1], has construed the word *Purusha* from its etymological roots, to connote an entity occupying a defined territory. The body is a limited physical territory, analogous to a city having nine exits[2]; and these nine exits or cavities consist of a pair of eyes, a pair of ears, a pair of nostrils; and the mouth, the anus and the penis, being the other three.

The *Samskrit* word *'Purusha'* literally means a person and denotes any creature. The creature is a dominion, a territory, having the defined outlets and extremities, and has, therefore, been metaphorically held as the simulant of a city, with a spirit ruling this city. Saint Augustine's *City of God,* has conceived the body pervaded by a divinity. The creature being, thus, a person, must also have a personality commensurate with its body. **The typical essence of a person is his personality** which stands for the classical behaviour of a creature; and since the behaviour of a creature is geared by the level of its consciousness, the *Upnishad*[3] is justified in describing the essence of a person as his consciousness, which is designated in *Samskrit* as *Vak*. The *Samskrit* word *Vaka* has numerous meanings including the vital force in the body, called by whatever name, as light, heat, electricity, fluid, breath or vibration, that animates and gives life to the body, and all these different words can be comprehended in the word 'consciousness'.

The word *Vak* is the metaphysical sense of speech, which is silent speech, a simple thought process, which

---

1. 8/4.
2. *Shwetashwaropnishad,* 3/18.
3. *Chhandogya Upnishad,* 1/1/2.

is a state of self-perception, more concretely, self-awareness. This state best synonymizes with the general comprehension of the term 'consciousness'.

Consciousness is practical experience derived by sense organs. The development of sense organs in all creatures not being same, the *Vak* or consciousness is an on-going process but different in different creatures, corresponding to the degree of perfection of their sense organs. In addition to the common attributes of all creatures, man is endowed also with intellect. **The intellect is the highest attainment within view of the cosmic process.**

This cosmic process operates through the five evolutes, namely, the *aakash*, air, fire and the earth. Earth, being the last evolute, has been conceived as the essence of the preceding four evolutes named above. Earth being the direct evolute of water, water has been denominated as the essence of earth. Water is the most active agent in the evolution of life. Formation of life is, therefore, due to hydraulic agency. The nutrients of the earth and the water both become responsible for the growth of vegetative stuff and vegetation is, therefore, the sap of water. Vegetation or the botanical life sustains the zoological life which has been correctly described as sap of vegetation. The first animal race was, therefore, purely herbivorous, the carnivorous race was the second or the third animal root. The animate life evolved out of inanimate matter, and the animate life became distinct from inanimate existence because of its consciousness, which is the reflective stage of an animate being. **The reflective stage is affirmed as the essence of life.**

Consciousness is the common property of animal life. It is by operation of consciousness that the animal becomes aware of itself. It is through consciousness that the animal perceives the effect of his motor and sense organs. The animal exists because it knows that it exists and it knows because it exists. **Thought is always unified with consciousness.**

Having set the order of animal life, the next in design of nature was to conceive certain values in life. The animal lives a life but a human being leads a life. Leading a life involves aims, ends, purposes, ambitions and goals.

The human life works in a system according to a scheme devised to achieve definite ends. Working in a system forbids arbitrariness. There is a plan in general which has deeper claims in the meaning of life and this meaning is discovered in the purpose for which life suffers and sustains. Life is not a race course of impulses in which attainments are let loose to exceed or supersede one another. Life is a systematic whole in which actions are modulated and tasks modelled.

It is a matter of diverging consequences whether the target or purpose is a social position, material prosperity or personal profit. The satisfaction of the person is the end of each activity. The person is a composite personality of numerous dimensions. The purpose of the person and the behaviour of his personality must conform to each other. In a larger perspective when men associate with each other, the individual behaviour has to conform to common disposition. A personal benefit has to submit to public good. The society assumes a personality and evolves a pattern of behaviour, and there is an altruistic purpose backing each social activity. Human good is based on conformity of the social behaviour with social purpose. Mankind becomes endowed with the realised idea of his own good and the good of his race.

The lower order of animals have although a self, the so-called soul, yet the self in the animal is only a striving but not a controlling self. The herd instinct in the animal has no social ethos, and no collective aim. Nature did not rest with the creation only of an order of life, devoid of intellectual acumen and spiritual percipience.

Even after setting an order of the animal kingdom, the quest of nature proceeded for a yet perfect figure to repose therein an extrinsic ethos in inward holiness.

Nature strived yet for a perfect figure with all organs fully equipped, in an impeccable life to which moral and spiritual values could be attributed. The contrivance of nature was thenceforth directed to concert life with moral rectitude and spiritual punctilio, which the animal world was left or kept without. The process of psychic evolution which so far ran parallel to physical evolution, culminated in the lower order with the infusion of consciousness, but ambled, thenceforth, to dress the apex life of man by inculcating therein the sense of intellectual and spiritual upliftment possible only in the human life deliberately organised and ordered with efficiency *ne plus ultra*, in the avowed juxtaposition and congruence of all its sense and motor organs.

The creation of a perfect life was the final handiwork of nature, as the *Aitereya Upnishad*[1] states that in the onward march for a really and immaculately perfect life, the nature initially presented the figure of a cow which was not found perfect, since it could not execute the design of nature to realise moral virtue and spiritual elevation. The figure of a horse was the next venture, but was rejected as equally imperfect. The final phase, then discovered the human figure, proved to be perfect for all the pre-requisites of nature.

The brevity of expression summarizing the process by naming only two quadrupeds is illustrative and not exhaustive. The terse statement is the clue to visualizing

1. 1/2/1-3.

the intricacies of the process in its entirety. These two represent the two notably popular quadrupeds, exhibiting the two elementary virtues of gentleness and bravery.

The above is complementary to the last two evolutes named in the *Chhandogya Upnishad*[1] as the culminating phase of evolution. The *Upnishad* described each succeeding evolutes as the quintessence of its predecessor. Starting from earth, the water is essence of earth. Water produces herbs, plants and cereals, and is essence of water. The person, which means any creature, is essence of vegetation, because it survives on edibles. The consciousness of creature is essence of its being. Consciousness is auxiliary to intellect. The intellect is essence of consciousness. The intellect makes the person aware of his values. The essence of intellect is stated to be the *Udgith,* which literally means the summit, the *Summum Bonum* of an onward march, and this onward march is for the end of self-realisation. **The man alone is capable to realise his spirit; and the purpose of nature having come to its fruition in the life of man, the evolutionary process was liable to enjoy its standstill.**

The word *Udgith* is a compound of three words, *Ut,* which means higher, *gi* which means going, and *th,* which means standstill.

The plenary existence is the vision of a spiritual life, a life of concord, equilibrium, harmony and oneness. This oneness is limitless. There is no higher end other than being one with the cosmic spirit, and such realisation is possible in human life alone. **Human life is the terminus of the process of psycho-physical evolution.**

The quest of nature was to procure a perfect frame of body. The strategy was to institute the best and the

1. 1/1/2.

superlative frame through which the cosmic spirit could be realised. The brutes cannot have moral sense since the mental faculty is less developed. The mind had itself to suffer so many stages in marching ahead from the brute consciousness to human consciousness. The human consciousness is a consciousness disciplined by moral virtue and spiritual values.

The lower and the higher, as orders of life, are only terms of evaluation which is possible only in the meditative life. The highest reach of the meditative life is one unqualified plenary existence immune from differences and limitations. Spiritual peace gets polluted by differences and limitations. The meditative life is beyond conflicts and contentions.

The meditative life is a rising stream of consciousness for perfect peace, which is an activity of progression through generation and re-generation of values. This is noted as a progression from brute nescience which was bound teleologically to realise its nature into fullest percipience of the self as integral part of the cosmos. This percipience realises its fullness of its reach through the successive ordering of life in conformity with the cosmic purpose. **The ordering process finds its tryst in the non-difference of the biological propensities with cosmic subtleties.**

The cosmic design in the gearing of life to its perfect physiognomy in the human being fulfills half of its purpose, and the remainder is for man to accomplish through his spiritual regeneration. It is through this regeneration that man becomes one with the cosmos. **The biological evolution after its standstill with the man, gives the process a turn for spiritual evolution.**

This explains perfectly well the standstill on advent of the man. Man is the turning point from psycho-physical evolution to ethico-spiritual evolution. Since man was the perfect creature, **the standstill on man is evidence of perfection.** Perfection is end of strivance and activity. The organic perfection of man is an end of biogenesis, yet the cosmic purpose was only half way, and the advent of man was a shift for another line of evolution, the intellectual, the moral and finally the spiritual.

The insight for this shift is for the residual complement of realising the spiritual reality. Flesh and appetite in fauna portrays only one epicycle of the evolutionary process. Man rich in intuition and intellect, then, must turn to the aspired goal of shedding away the flesh again and survive as unsullied spiritual entity as integral part of the cosmic spirit. Short of this, there was no reason to endow man with intuition and intellect which the lower order was deprived of. Man may suffer and depart from his carnal frame, but the spirit survives in cosmic space and the interregnum between death and rebirth may be long or short or instant, commensurate with his actions and impulses. This is the immutable law writ large on the process exhorting man to overcome the cycle of births and deaths, and stay eternally in the cosmos as a spiritual entity. It is for the variegated experience that the spirit assumes a fleshy form, for its final retreat unto the cosmic spirit. Just as on death, the constituents of the fleshy frame dissolve into their corresponding elements, so the spirit, too, must, sooner or later, find its anchor in the cosmic spirit.

The evolutionists could lay down empirical but volatile theories, failing to explain the art of procreation.

5.2 Account of Procreation

Procreation is outcome of instinctive coitus between a male and a female counterpart of the same species. **Creation, hence, perceptibly precedes procreation,** since procreation posits a point of standstill in the origin of species, one or the other being irrelevant.

Ever since the creature mastered the art of procreation, all thereafter slided to a facile process on seed to seed basis, and if each species is doomed to beget its like, there is no role for any supposed evolution of one preceding race into any other succeeding race, and evolution as so conceived becomes oblivious.

Creation as the preceding agent of procreation, is an endless permutation of life patterns in the cosmic space.

The cosmos is full of life, the cosmic space is an unfathomable reservoir of life. Each particle of space is a constituent of life. There is constant flow of life from the cosmic vault down to the earth giving the material shape to the patterns.

Life comes on earth in terms of forms, models, patterns or types moulded on subtle imperceptible matter, each serving as specimen or archetype, instilled into the earth which incubated them and developed a tangible body fitting with the pattern. The process of developing an idea into a perceptible body is the responsibility of the earth. This impregnation of the earth is creation whereby the earth succeeded in delivering a complete body in conformity with the basic pattern devised by the cosmic libido, known in the *Vedic* literature the *Kama*[1]. **The procreation starts when the creature delivered by the earth is provided with its counterpart female.**

Procreation is only an off-shoot of creation, and the *Kama* as contemplated in the *Rigveda* is the innate cosmic urge, metaphysically conceived as the Eros or the Libido, the intrinsic impulse of the cosmic spirit to issue forth into creation. The purpose was to make manifest what was

1. *Rigveda,* 10/129.

unmanifest, that is, to release its energy and realise its potentiality. Sex is the gross manifestation of the cosmic Eros, depicted in the Hindu mythology as cupid or the *Kama Deva*, no less than a divinity. Procreation is a pious act of any creature and sex is adored, by human beings as an aim to preserve the species. Progeny must be multiplied, says the *Taittiriyopnishad*[1]. Since multiplicity of species requires sufficient foodstuff, the *Taittiriyopnishad*[2] has recommended more and more growth of cereals.

The fact remains that procreation requires a dual act, not possible to be performed by one alone[3]. **The origin of female is the most occult question.**

5.3 Origin of Female

It is futile to cavil whether the egg came first or the hen. There is no illusion of such sort in the *Vedic* philosophy. The cosmic metaphysics conceives a cosmic egg in the beginning. The entire creation is egg-born. In the beginning there was the egg[4], a golden egg, known as *Brahmanda* or the *Hiranyagarbha*. The *Ishavasyopnishad*[5] names it as a golden pot. There is a specific *hymn* in the *Rigveda*[6] in the name of *Hiranyagarbha Sukta*.

Taking the theory of the Big Bang, in the beginning there was all a canopy of darkness. The theory has its origin in the *Rigveda*[7] which affirms a deep abyss of darkness in the beginning, and there was no life.

The birth of fire from the element of air itself derived from the element of *aakash*, is the event named by

1. 2/6/4.
2. 3/9.
3. *Brihadaranyak Upnishad,* 1/4/3.
4. *Manusmriti,* 1/9-12.
5. *Hymn,* 15.
6. 10/121.
7. 10/129.

scientists as the Big Bang. The Big Bang simply explains the birth of Sun, which, in the *Vedic* metaphysics is *Hiranyagarbha* or the golden egg. The birth of the Sun denotes the point of time of origin of life. In the *Hiranyagarbha Sukta* of the *Rigveda*, the Sun is described as the fountain of life, and the Lord of all born creatures. The stage before the origin of fire, was absence of life. Life originates from solar energy. The darkness preceding the origin of Sun was state of dissolution or the cosmic death. It is a state of deep cosmic slumber stated mythologically as the *Yoganidra*.[1]

This state of cosmic slumber is the incubative state. The egg erupts when fully incubated, and becomes the origin of life both male and female. The first stage of life was epicenic which erupted into two heterosexual entities, in the same way as an egg should irrupt. This epicenic image has been aptly represented in the mythological artefact of the *Ardhanarishwar*, that is, the hermaphrodite god. This metaphysical concept when manifested into gross physical action, gave rise to another symbol of the *Shivling*. Both these symbol represent a transition from the hermaphrodite unity to the heterosexual duality. **Life has no bias for gender. The male and the female have issued from the original neuter gender having double potentiality.**

Holding that the theory of monogenesis as well as the descent of man from the mammals as mistaken and fatal to the completeness of evolutionary theories, Madam H. P. Blavatsky[2] quotes from Darwin's *Descent of Men*[3], the following passage which would show how near Darwin had been to the *Vedic* theory of the universal law in

---

1. See *Markandeya Purana, Durga Saptashati*, Ch.-I, verses 84-89.
2. The Secret Doctrines, 7th Adyar Edn., Vol.-II, p.118.
3. Second Edition, 1875, Ch.-VI, p. 161.

physical evolution, acting indifferently in the construction of plants, animals and men:

> "It has long been known in the vertebrate kingdom that one sex bears rudiments of various accessory parts, appertaining to the reproduction system which properly belongs to the opposite sex, hence some remote progenitor of the whole vertebrate kingdom appears to have been hermaphrodite or androgynous. But here we encounter singular difficulty. In the mammalian class, the males possess rudiments of a uterus with the adjacent passes in the *vesiculae prostaticae*, they bear also rudiments of *mammae*, and some male marsupials have traces of marsupial sack. Other analogous facts could be added. Are we then to support that some extremely ancient mammals continued androgynous, after it has acquired the chief distinctions of the class, and, therefore, after it has diverged from the lower class of the vertebrate kingdom? This seems very improbable, for we have to look to fishes, the lowest of all classes to find any still existent androgynous form."

The scriptures testify, and rightly so, that the first embodied organism was a hermaphrodite or an epicenic corpus, that is, an incubated heat potential, a monistic principle, which later on bisected itself into its male and female counterparts, by its inner impulsion of Eros, euphemized in the *Rigveda*[1] as the *Kama*. The term *Kama* connotes a principle whereas sex is an act, known in *Samskrit* as *Rati*, the consort of *Kama Deva*, the god of evil since conceived in the *Bible* and the *Quran* as *Satan*. It is a serpentine force which excites the body from top to bottom. The *Bible*[2] has rightly depicted it as serpent. In

1. 10/129.
2. The *Genesis*.

the *Purana* literature, Lord *Shiva* had immolated this force and the serpentine force could not agitate Him. The anguine species are, thus, depicted as the creeping ornaments on the body of Lord *Shiva*.

A Hindu legendric deity is *Ardhanarishwar*, the androgynous god, having both male and female symptoms, integrally compact into one another.

The symbol explains the theme that unless the male and the female aspects were not present in the same organism, the organism could reproduce only either male or female. The birth of male and female is one single incident. The creative force bisected the hermaphrodite into two heterosexual bodies. The principle finally became practice, and the one original couple of the bisected male and female, then, procreated the offsprings by mutual union. Creation by reproduction then became a natural practice and creatures were reproducing each by the union of its male and female parents.

It becomes evident that the first born, that is the nature born hermaphrodite, could neither be exclusively male nor exclusively female but had to be both, so that future progeny gets on by birth of males and females both.

It was, therefore, logical necessity to trace the origin of the male and the female to a single source. The incubated heat potential of the androgynous principle gets bifurcated by its inner erotic propulsion and the one, thereafter, splits up into the two[1]. 'Let me have my lady', says the *Brihadaranyak Upnishad*[2]; and whenever the two, thus, form a couple, they fulfill each other's desire[3]. In order that the covetous also becomes cohabitous, a

1. *Prashnopnishad*, 1/4.
2. 1/4/7.
3. *Chhandogya Upnishad*, 1/1/6.

bifurcation was inevitable, since the one alone cannot copulate as the *Brihadaranyak Upnishad*[1] clarifies. According to the *Brihadaranyak Upnishad*[2], the one hermaphrodite, as compact as a cereal, split apart, and became man and wife. The *Purana* literature asserts this theory frequently enough.

The birth of *Saraswati* bifurcated from *Brahma* is alluded to in the *Matsyapurana*. The *Markandeya Purana*[3] refers this event of bifurcation in triple order, that is, three different hermaphrodites reproducing three sets of men and women. In the Hindu mythology, these couples are counted as the *Brahma* and the *Saraswati*, the *Vishnu* and the *Laxmi* and the *Shiva* and the *Parvati*. These three are the first bifurcated entities from one stem.

The *Genesis*[4] has stated the same event differently:

> "The Lord caused a deep sleep to fall upon *Adam*, and he select, and he took some of his ribs and closed up the flesh instead thereof; and the rib the Lord had taken from man, made he a woman, and..."

The meaning of 'deep sleep' denotes the point before the stage of bisection which was a state of dormancy and they became active only after bisection.

Madam H. P. Blavatsky[5] says with reference to the names of certain scholars to have taught that *Adam* had two faces and one person, and from the beginning, he was both male and female, male on one side and female on the other, like *Manu*'s *Brahma*[6], but afterwards the parts have separated.

1. 1/4/3.
2. 1/4/1-3.
3. *See* Durga Saptashati, Murti Rahasya.
4. 2/22.
5. The Secret Doctrines, 7th Adyar Edn., Vol.-II, p.134-135.
6. *Manusmriti*, 1/9-12.

A Psalm of David[1] states:

"Thou hest fashioned me behind and before."

This is evidence again of the truth that the primeval form of mankind was androgynous. The *Manusmriti*[2] verifies that 'by dividing his body into two he became a man with one and a woman with the other half.'

In the *Vishnu Purana*[3], *Prithu,* the first known King on earth is said to have been churned out, by *Brahmins,* from the thigh of *Vena,* whom the *Brahmins* had killed because of his arrogance. The incident refers to a manual process of bifurcation of an organism into two.

The *Durga Saptashati,* in the *Markandeya Purana* refers to a demon, named, *Raktabeej* from whose droplets of blood could generate an identical clone of him. However, cloning is different from bifurcation. In the beginning there could be no cloning and the advent of the male and female counterparts could be possible only through bifurcation.

The concept of Big Bang is itself the theory of eruption of the cosmic egg and eruption is simple bifurcation. **In the process of eruption, the envelop of the egg simply bifurcates.**

The scientists believe that there have been numerous bangs, but one or many makes no difference, since each bang is result of an eruption.

The heterogeneity of sex, or bisexuality appeared only as a result of the event of bifurcation, or the eruption of the cosmic egg. What remains after eruption of the egg is the golden yolk. This golden yolk of the cosmic egg has been depicted as personified and deified in the form of

---

1. *Hymn,* 139.
2. 1/32-33.
3. 1/13/25-37.

the deity of *Brahma*, the Creator Lord, the originator of life, perceptibly the Sun.

Botany is evidence of bifurcation. The seed is compact unity of two equal halves which bifurcate to ooze out in the sprout which originally buds out into two leaves. The branches bifurcate themselves from the stem. The fruit, flowers and leaves, again, illustrate the process of bifurcation, that is a new entity sprouting out from the original. The ocular biological instance of bifurcation is the earthworm which bisects itself into two linear forms *de hors* the sex.

The bifurcation, fertilization and multiplication of the life cells in the body bears the same rule of one entity giving rise to two, and the two then get united again for carrying on the line of procreation. Bifurcation was biological necessity for bringing the creation down on seed to seed basis. Bifurcation is, therefore, cosmic law from the androgynous mass down to the minute component cells of the body, the rule remains the same, that is, bifurcation and multiplication.

The androgynous mass bifurcates and the two when united, then, start procreation on seed to seed basis. The seed is again a compact of the male and the female counterpart, that is, the sperm of the man and the ovum of the woman and the seed because of its hermaphrodite character can be born either a male or a female in proportion to the polarity of the male and female forces in the hermaphrodite. The instinct was Eros. After bifurcation, the Eros manifests into sex.

The legendric epicene in the symbol of *Ardhanarishwar*, that is, male and female compact, and another symbol of the *Shiva ling*, that is, a phallus projected into a vagina, conveys the process in between the bifurcation and procreation, on seed to seed basis. Heterosexuality is generated from bisexuality.

The above exegesis can be summarised into the following palpably acceptable conclusion:

1. The first nature-born creature was a dormant mass of matter and was potentially a hermaphrodite and this is true of any creature.
2. The dormant in that hermaphrodite mass, brought into it, by law of nature, a conscious life with the faculties of knowing, willing and feeling.
3. The one composite hermaphrodite product was, of course, not a lifeless organism since a lifeless mass of matter can have no inner agitation so as to split into two. Splitting into two is an activity alien to an inanimate body. The dormancy of the first born was not total inaction but was the state only of listlessness in as much as it was besot by a doubly active Eros, and the light of life crept into him moments before the event of bisection.
4. Since the first born never came from an embryo, it can be assumed that it were never in an infantile size but was full blown person.
5. The first sensation occurring to the first born was that of self awareness which made it to utter 'this is I'[1] and the first feeling that filled this figure was that of fear since the one alone must fear[2] but seeing that there was no other to be afraid of, he was relieved of his fear but instantly then he became overwhelmed by sexual urge; and since he was single, it was not possible to satisfy his lust, with the result that he disposed his figure in a form of man and woman embraced together, like the two parts of a cereal

1. *Brihadaranyak Upnishad,* 1/4/1.
2. *Ibid.,* 1/4/2.

compact in one; and, finally, he divided his figure, into two of man and woman respectively; and as sage *Yajnavalkya* says, the 'figure of a creature two-in-one'[1].

6. There is some anomaly in the portrayal of the hermaphrodite figure. In the portrayal of the ideal of the *Ardhanarishwar*, the figure has been depicted as male on the left and a female on the right half. In the *Psalm* of David[2], the compact figure was described as two in front and behind. In the *Brihadaranyak Upnishad*[3], the two-in-one has been depicted as embracing each other, face to face. Then, again, in the *Brihadaranyak Upnishad*[4], the first born was originally one and the other was a later projection when it was overwhelmed by sex. There being ocular testimony of the exact position of the first born prior to its bisection, the difference in the portrayal of the epicenic figure need not create quandary, since the bisection, in either case was, and could only be, vertical.

7. According to the *Brihadaranyak Upnishad*[5] the first instinct which beset the first born was that of fear; and the next which immediately followed was that of sex[6]. As regards the instinct of hunger, the *Upnishad*[7] has identified it with death. The birth of the first born was in consequence of the impulsion of death to become incarnate. The *Upnishad*, therefore,

1. *Ibid.*, 1/4/3.
2. 139/5.
3. 1/4/3.
4. *Ibid.*
5. 1/4/2.
6. *Ibid.*, 1/4/3.
7. *Ibid.*, 1/2/4-5.

unambiguously holds death as the cause of birth. The *Upnishad* states:

> "It desired to bring forth its another body and so it desired a duplicate in the form of twins. It then agaped, that is, opened its mouth towards the first born to swallow it, and the first born, in turn, made an exclamation which exclamation became the first spoken word.'
>
> 'Thence it thought that if it would kill that first born, it would procure just little food; and eventually created the animate and the inanimate objects and thought of eating whatever it produced; and whatever one ate, became its food."

The above statement, rhetoric or esoteric, seeks to describe the onset of a sort of appetite, and it was this appetite which operated simultaneously both as hunger and sex. This is what can be deduced in plane logical terms from this terse diction. **Fear, hunger and sex, thus, appear to be the three master instincts which beset the first born in a consecutive simultaneity**.

This explains the origin of all the four categories of species, the egg-born, the womb-born, the soil-born and the sweat-born recognised in the Hindu theory of genetics.

The question as now survives is to consider the order of origin of species.

6. Order of Origin of Species

In the process of physical evolution, water having been prior to earth, it follows that aquatic life must have preceded all other kinds of life. According to the *Genesis*, the first in order of biogenesis was the aquatic life which was followed by the avian life. The *Genesis*[1] states:

---

1. 1/20-22.

> "20. And God said, let the waters bring forth abundantly the moving creatures that hath life, and fowl, that may fly above the earth in the open firmament of heaven.'
>
> '21. And God created great whales and every living creature that moveth, which the waters brought forth abundantly, after their kind, and every winged fowl after his kind; and God saw that it was good.'
>
> '22. And God blessed them, saying, be fruitful, and multiply and fill the waters in the seas and let fowl multiply in the earth."

The expression 'after their kind' is strong evidence of reproduction, negating the fallacious proposition of one particular species developing or evolving into another.

As regards the origin of species on land, the *Genesis* is clear in affirming the priority of origin of the plant species. The *Genesis*[1] maintains:

> "11. And God said, let the earth bring forth grass, the herb yielding seed, and the fruit, tree yielding fruit, after his kind, whose seed is in itself upon the earth; and it was so.'
>
> '12. And the earth brought forth grass and herb yielding seed after his kind and the tree yielding fruit, whose seed was in itself, after his kind."

Scriptures are liable to differ on one or the other point, but the fundamentals which they agree upon, must stay as gospel truth.

The Hindu scriptures testify the fact that the aquatic species were the first in point of time.

The incarnation or the *Avatar* theory of the *Purana* literature, reckons the origin of life in the fish, as is

1. 1/11-12.

evident from the *Matsya Purana* which is an episode on the birth of the fish.

The *Avatar* theory is, in terms, a simple explanation of the modes or strides in which the life principle had assumed its physical forms; and according to the *Matsya Purana*, the life principle became incarnate first of all in the form of a fish. The next is *Koorma Purana*, that is, the episode on the tortoise, which vouches that the fish race was, in due course, followed by the tortoise race. The fish and the tortoise are just two representative species of the aquatic life, and the tortoise following the fish carries the plausible surmise that the creatures having flexible and delicate shell were followed, later, by creatures having tough and stout shell. It was neither possible nor feasible to describe the origin of each and every aquatic creatures, and a reference only to the two representative aquatic species was sufficient to summaries the biogenesis in the aquatic world.

There is no specific reference to the origin of avian species in the *Upanishads*. In the *Yajurveda*[1] the order of origin of species is general and too laconic as regards origin of avian, wild and domestic creatures but in the *hymn*, the terms used can conveniently be transposed, and no priority can be ascribed among the avian species and the mammalia.

In the perennial belief of *Vedic* cosmogenesis, life has been traced to a cosmic egg, and since the cosmos itself is born from egg, the genesis of the oviparous species can be conceived as the first in point of time, more so when the aquatic species as the first in point of time, both in the *Bible*[2] as well as in the Hindu epics, is accepted to be the first in point of time.

---

1. 31/1.
2. The *Genesis*.

Therefore, the origin of the avian species can be placed in between the aquatic and the mammalian species.

The *Chhandogya Upnishad*[1] has delineated the process from the flora to the fauna. The *Bhagwadgita*[2] attributes the biogenesis to the cereals and the version in the *Manusmriti*[3] is the same. Thus, the botanical species preceded the zoological species. The egg-born must have preceded the womb-born for the reason that the vegetative world had itself grown in stages and could not have bloomed up all at once. The smaller creatures of avian species required scanty food and must have emerged first in point of time. The bipeds and quadrupeds must have emerged when the produce of cereal became plentiful, so as to suffice even for the mammoth pachyderm.

The tale of origin of the biped from the brute is interesting. According to the *Purana* literature, the *Narsingha Purana* takes a leap to launch the origin of a leonine species, with the head of lion and torso of a man, a strange combination of strength and industry.

The head of lion represents strength and beastliness of wild life whereas the hands of the figure represent industry. This epic seems to introduce the origin of absurd species, but found to be rare, coming out accidentally without prevision. It appears that such anomalous creatures could not generate a seed to multiply their kind. These rare figures were taken with awe and became objects of worship, obviously because they once existed as a single specimen. **They could not procreate, and became extinct.** The race exists by reason

1. 1/1/2.
2. 3/14.
3. 3/76.

of procreation. Similar is the case of another idol of Lord *Ganesha* with the head of an elephant, and the torso of man, followed by two other amazing idols of the *hayagreeva*, having the head of a horse fixed on the torso of a man, and that of *Kakbhushundi*, having the head of a crow fixed on the torso of a man. The origin of such rare pieces of life has no explanation accept the freak or accident of nature. Since they could not procreate, they stayed as rare, and were adored as an uncommon instance of life.

May be, this was some experiment contemplated by nature and, then having found that the product was of no utility, it separated the bipeds from the quadrupeds into two specialized species. **Experience by trial and error is open to any creative agency.**

The incarnation of human life has been alluded to in the *Vamana Purana*. The word '*Vamana*' literally means a pigmy, dwarf or the homunculus. The allusion takes into account an anecdote of winning over a Demon King named *Bali*, by a dwarf. The incarnate dwarf begged of the King to donate him a strip of land equal to three steps as be taken by the beggar dwarf. The gift being granted, the dwarf turned into a mammoth size and measured out the entire earth only within his two steps with the result that the King had to offer his own head for the third step, of the dwarf to ambulate on. The King was nonplussed and was, thus, overpowered. The symbolic insinuation of the anecdote are inexplicable, except the conclusion that the descent of man on earth followed the origin of the bizarre wild species, having animal head and a human torso, like the *Narshingha*, the *Ganesha*, the *Hayagreeva*, etc.

Be that as it may, that the first human form might have been a homunculus, developing, in course of ages, to its average size, the fact remains that the animal race in their origin had preceded the human race, as evidenced in the *Aitereyopnishad*[1] stating that the Lord Creator created a cow which the principle of a superlative life rejected as deficient so that the Creator, then presented the form of a horse which, too, was dissented from, so as to finally inspire the Creator to come forward with the human figure, which the life motif accepted as perfect as well as excellent. There is consensus in the *Genesis* and the *Purana* literature read with the *Aitereya Upnishad* that the origin of human species had followed the origin of animal species. There is slight difference between the view in the *Purana* and in the *Aitereya Upnishad* on the point that whereas the *Vamana Purana* contemplates the birth of a homunculus as the first human stripling, and that, too, after the origin of the leonine form, the *Aitereya Upnishad* traces the descent of man after the bovine and the equestrian species.

The *Vamana* or the homunculus is, of course, different from those bizarre species as the *Ganesha*, *Narsingha*, etc., which may not be species and might have been projected only as ideals representing the basal animality in any human being, and, thus, the head of that particular animal was projected upon a human figure in order simply to denote a particular beastly nature or tendency. But the *Vamana* was a full dress human being but very short in structure. Gulliver's voyage to Lilliput, reminds of such *Vamana* species. No wonder, the first race of human beings might be of Lilliputians.

The *Purana* is compilation of eighteen treatises and it is difficult to ascertain their order in point of time. The theme common to all is the origin of the universe, each tracing the origin to some particular potentiality of

---

1. 1/2/1-3.

nature, with the conclusion that each manifest form has its roots in one or the other particular force of nature. A probe into the metaphysical meaning of the episode would reveal that there has been some progressive order in the origin of species. The species manifested by a superior agency of nature, attained a superior form or comparatively a better or perfect form.

In the *Varaha Purana*, which is a treatise on the origin of the boar species. Whereas the *Narsingha Purana* has traced the origin from the leonine species, the *Varaha Purana* has traced it from the swine species. All this is anthromorphic analysis of the terse tenets of origin of life from the cosmic life principle in a way that the predominance of one or the other potentialities of nature lead to the predominance of an accessory in the resultant organism. This anthromorphic device has been adopted in order to make an interesting reading of the otherwise lough principles of metaphysics.

There is an agreement in the *Purana* that species have appeared on earth in conformity with a plan or design inherent in nature. The differences, if any are minor but not on material points. The editing of these different treatises being associated with different ages, it is not possible to appreciate the exact order or sequence of time consumed in the transition from one to the other species.

The nature has unlimited creativity, and there can be no exact figure to denote each and every species. The nature does it at its will and is free to change, modify, multiply or extinguish any species. The treatises in the *Purana* are rhetoric and full of imagery. The principle summarised by the *Chhandogya Upnishad*[1] is a definite statement that the combination of water and soil was responsible for origin of any species; and that animal life

1. 1/1/2.

has come out of vegetable life, and human life is an outcome of animal life.

In the manufactory of a smith, there are wares and wares, simple as well as sophisticated, fabricated in the pattern idealized by the smith. The cosmofactory has been at work in creating patterns of life at its own choice. **What the nature wills cannot be impeded.**

The *Ramayana* age of the Hindu civilization consisted of different and distinct races of human beings, spread over the territory from northern India upto Srilanka. The *Aryan*, the *Nishada*, the *Rakshasa*, and the *Vanara* were the prominent human species. In the *Mahabharata* period, there is no mention of the *Rakshasa* and the *Vanara* races. A race of *Nag* species, is known both in the *Ramayana* and the *Mahabharata* period. The *Manusmriti*[1] has named specific global human races, named as the *Paundraka, Audra, Kamboj, Yavana, Shaka, Parada, Palhava, China, Kirata, Darada* and *Khasha*.

This is evidence of the fact that whereas the races have differed, the species have remained the same. These are the patterns of human form, developed under different physiological and physiographical circumstances.

Whereas the bizarre patterns of the *Narsingha* or *Ganesha*, etc., might be errors or experiments of the nature, there is authentic reference in the *Purana* literature to the divine incarnations, known as the *Avatar*. The word *Avatar* literally means to become incarnate. The embodiment of life on earth may have traced its ingredients from the superlative forces of nature, thereby giving birth to the superhuman persons, having no parallel in that particular age, as are the *Rama* and the *Krishna*, worshipped as superhuman persons.

1. 10/44.

The primeval *Avatars* were instances of transition from wild to the civil race, after descent of man and since settlement of humanity, the *Avatar* miracle started creating supermen.

All that is an account of how the forces and ingredients of nature have combined in the formation of the particular species or a particular or even an illustrative person also in the human species.

The world is the habitat of myriads or creatures, man, animal, worms, insects, reptiles and the imperceptible bacteria, and the moot question is to get at the principle responsible for the typical differences in the pattern of species.

7. Moot Question

The one perennial faith of the *Vedic* cosmology is an explanation of the formation of the different patterns for bearing the same life principle. In the legends, the number of different species has been spread upto 84 lakhs, but that is only a limit set on the process of calculation, and cannot be a ceiling on the number. The point is that the number is countless.

There is an agency in nature named as the *Brahmanspati*[1], constantly busy with the function of moulding the patterns of life in the same way as a blacksmith moulds his wares by his bellows. The nature is ceaselessly busy with the routine function of moulding patterns or forms of life, and there was no reason to stop the process of creation altogether, even after the advent of the human race.

There is a law which keeps this cosmofactory in action, and that law is the law of Karma and rebirth.

---

1. *Rigveda,* 10/72.

CHAPTER 5

KARMA AND REBIRTH

SYNOPSIS

1. Concept of life
2. Death and Rebirth
3. Relativity of Space and Time
4. Two Tracks and the Law of *Karma*
5. Conclusion

1. Concept of life

Literally, the word 'life' denotes the condition that distinguishes animals and plants from inorganic objects. The characteristics of life are:

(i) Growth through metabolism;

(ii) Reproduction; and

(iii) Power of adaptation to environment through changes originating internally.

From metaphysical point of view, the cosmos is replete with life, which is not life construed in the sense of temporal life. What permeates the cosmos is not life in the mundane sense but the life principle which operates in a given physical frame. The mundane life can, thus, be defined as the survival of a being from point of time of its birth to the point of time of its death, which duration of existence is reckoned as the span of life or the longevity, and the period intervening these two points, is the calendar of life of a being.

The mundane life consists of the life principle pervading a given organism which is a composite mass of the five elements of nature, namely, the *aakash*, the air, the fire, and the earth, commingled in definite shape formed in its appropriate cuts and curves. This outer frame encasing the life principle, is a lump of flesh stuffed on a skeletal frame, with a skin coated thereon, though this skeletal bony structure may be absent in case of small insects. This physical frame is an apparatus consisting of bones, flesh and blood and identifies the class or kind of life known as the species.

The temporal life, thus, stands for the inherence of the life principle in a physical accoutrement, known as the body. Conversely, the exit of the life principle is death. The aftermath of death delineates the demise of the body and the departure therefrom of the life principle. This indicates an idea responsible for determining the forms, patterns or models of bodies serving as the rendezvous of the life principle till a stipulated time, making a basis for rebirth.

2. Death and Rebirth

In the *Brihadaranyak Upnishad*[1], sage *Pravahan* explains to his disciple, *Gautam*, that on completion of the given longevity of a person, he dies, and, on his death, they (the relatives) take the dead to the sacred-fire, and consign the deceased to his funeral pyre, with the result that the fire of his body gets dissolved into the cosmic fire, and, likewise, all other constituents of his immolated body get dissolved into the corresponding elements of nature.

All constituents of the body are cremated in the consecrated fire, but the life principle stays and has to traverse its course to its heavenly abode. The *Chhandogya Upnishad*[2], then, refers to two specific tracks for the

1. 6/2/14; see also *Chhandogya Upnishad*, 5/3/3.
2. 5/10/2-10.

osmosis of the life principle upto the heavens, one the right track, known as the *Devyan*, that is, the divine track, and the other, the left track, known as the *Pitrayan* or the ancestorial course. The virtuous go on the *Devyan* track but the mediocres automatically turn to the *Pitrayan* track. It is stated later[1] that the vile and the depraved are not allowed on either track but loiter in the biosphere and, being nearest to earth, they are liable to be reborn instantly or within reasonable time. The *Upnishad* has explained these propositions.

The life principle automatically recoils into the cosmic life, in the same way as the elemental stuff of *aakash*, air, fire, water and earth are relegated to their original elemental state.

In the *Chhandogya Upnishad*[2], the question is posed: *why is it that despite recurring deaths on the earth, the cosmic space is never over-crowded*?

The answer is that the departed soul is reborn again through a scientific process, and the cycle of deaths and rebirths continues without rest and neither the space above gets over-crowded nor the earth here gets over-loaded.

These two tracks are two opposite points, two points of polarity, maintaining the circuit of cosmic gravitation. This explains the significance of two opposite tracks.

The theory of two tracks explains the relativity of space and time.

3. Relativity of Space and Time

Geographers have conceived the terrestrial globe as divided into the North and the South hemispheres. On the same analogy, the astronomers have conceived the

1. *Chhandogya Upnishad*, 5/10/7.
2. 5/3/3.

heavenly vault into the North and the South solstices, named each as an *Ayan*, the northern solstice named as *Uttarayana* and the southern solstice as the *Dakshiayana*. The position of the Earth having the Sun in the north of the Equator is the *Uttarayana*, and the converse of it, when the Sun goes down the Equator, the solstice is *Dakshiayana*. The two taken together denote the completion of a year termed as the *Samvatsar*.

There appears to be no legitimate synonym in the English language for the term *ayan*. It can be synonymised with the word *'annal'* but in the *Vedic* sense, this *'annal'*, or the 'annual' periodicity, is not a vacuous entity but a reality. It is part of the cosmic game. The game starts with the pulsating moment of the temporal reality, capable of being multiplied upto epochs. It is roughly measured, on human convenience, in the temporal parameter of years. The one annual parameter is one *Samvatsar*. The reality of time endures till the cosmos endures. When the cosmos is dissolved, the time withers away and restarts conterminously with the onset of the solar system. The pulse of the cosmos is the throb of the Sun. The Sun is a throbbing mass of active energy; and energy being name of dynamicity, it is spontaneous with any energy to be throbbing. This throbbing is evident in the human body, causing constant inhalation and exhalation of the breath. **The continuity of throbbing is the consciousness of duration of time.**

Life departs from body on the last beat of this throb. Measured immeasurably, there is time also for a last breath destining the cosmos as a whole to dissolve; and then time begins to run afresh coextensively with the fresh creation.

The phenomenon of time is termed in the *Vedic* philosophy as the *Kala* which is a companion of the cosmos, and each creation and dissolution, practically stands for life and death of the cosmos. Time can be conceived as the functional aspects of energy representing a force. **Energy and force are one, and the moment of its activisation is the commencement of time, coextensive with cosmogenesis.**

The convenient way of computation of time is with reference to days and years. The diurnal rotation of the planet on its axis, and its annual revolution round the Sun, represent respectively a day and a year. The annual revolution is commensurate with the flight of the planet on its orbit, and this orbit is the line of control of the motion of the planet determining the speed of the planet. The speed of the planet on its orbit provides the mathematics of time and the period consumed by the planet in completing its revolution round the Sun, is reckoned as the year for that planet. Each planet is liable to compute its own year relatively to the year of another planet. This sums up the real theory of relativity of space and time. **Einstein's theory of relativity is one aspect of the *Vedic* theory of relativity.**

The *Samskrit* word *Samvatsar* is the calculation of the period taken by a planet in completing its revolution round the Sun. The *Samvatsar* when divided into two halves, each half would be an *ayan*. The orbit of the planet accordingly becomes divided into two parts which are not parts but divisions of the orbit of the planet. When the Sun is in the North of the planet it is *Uttarayana* or the divine track whereas when the Sun is in the South of the planet, it is *Dakshiayana*, in relation to the planet.

A departed soul is directed to one or the other track on merits of its actions. **The cumulative abstract of the actions of man becomes itself a unit of force, or a gravity of its own, since each action presupposes the exertion of some force and each exertion generates its**

own quantum of gravitation. Whereas on the one hand, the gravitational line of control keeps the balance among the planets, the same force attracts the unit of gravitation abstracted from a balance of the individual's actions in his life. If the balance sheet is excellent the soul is caught gravitationally by the divine track, but if fairly good, the soul is gravitationally thrown on the ancestorial track. If the balance sheet is bad, both the tracks are denied, and the departed soul lounges in the biosphere to be born within no time or within reasonable time. The metaphysics of the two tracks explains the Law of *Karma*.

4. Two Tracks and the Law of *Karma*

The cosmos is sustained by gravitational balance. The two tracks contemplated in the *Chhandogya Upnishad*, are gravitational pulls of one point against another operating in a circuit. This circuit represents the Law of *Karma*. The balance of good and bad actions accumulated in the whole span of life of an individual being, becomes a force in itself. The commissions and omissions on the part of a man, are ephemeral, but the effect they produce is eternal. It is at once recorded in the balance sheet of the departed soul and the soul is automatically attracted and taken on the *Devyan* track, if the balance sheet is marked as virtuous, and, likewise, if the balance leans or indicates towards mediocrity, the dead soul is taken up on the *Pitrayan* track; and all this is an eternal cycle in which the law of *karma* operates. The Law of *Karma* is a force operating on gravitational laws. The soul would be thrown to its appropriate track on merit of its individual *Karma*, and the cosmic *Karma* picks and chooses the souls for either track on basis of quantum of gravity of individual actions, taken cumulatively.

This balance sheet is given the name of *Samskara*, in the *Vedic* philosophy.

The cosmos itself has its life and is liable to dissolve in the same way as a dead body. **The cosmos is bound by the collective *karma* of the previous creation, and the collective *karma* of the current term of the cosmos will determine the subsequent creation. The individual self is bound by this immutable cosmic law and determines his life on rebirth on the merit of his actions done in the past life.** This is the law of *karma* stated in simplest terms.

The *Chhandogya Upnishad*[1] proceeds to describe the onward journey of the departed soul after it has taken the prescribed track. Having taken one of these tracks, the departed soul gets into the diurnal force of the universe which are responsible for the causation of day and nights. Thenceforth, the soul proceeds higher and joins the force which causes the fortnights. Thereafter, the soul comes up to the North solstice, and becomes part of the annual time, called *Samvatsar*. Thereafter, the soul proceeds towards the solar disc and thenceforth to the lunar disc, and, finally, to the lightening zone where there is an impersonal entity which elevates this ongoing micro-life principle up to the active macro-principle of life.

The *Chhandogya Upnishad*[2] has described this journey to and fro these two tracks, in succinct terms. Supposing the departed soul proceeds via the divine track, it has its halt on the *Samvatsar*.[3] The next halt is around the solar disc and the third, around the lunar disc, and then to an abstract force which destines them to return.

Those who get to the second or the ancestorial track, stay in the smoke, then into the night, then into the black

1. 5/10/1-2.
2. 5/10.
3. *See* under heading-3, supra.

fortnight and thereafter into the region when the Sun is *Dakshiayana*[1] in relation to the planet. These souls have no sojourn on the *Samvatsar*. Thence forward, these souls go to the abode of the ancestors and thereafter dwell in the yonder space, and then get to the region of the Moon. The Moon is the stuff which the gods feed upon.

The time determined by the balance sheet of the past actions, the souls stay and return on the same way. They come to the *aakash*, from *aakash* to the air, from air to the smoke, from smoke to cloud, from cloud to the rain, and, finally, from rain to the cereal. This particular cereal which the particular soul becomes in this process, is ultimately consumed by the same creature from whom the soul was destined to be born. The departed soul on its return journey is transformed into the form of a corn and is consumed by some other creature, and the creature who consumes it causes the rebirth of that particular soul. The rebirth migrates in the same species who had consumed the cereal which were the last remains at the last terminus of the departed soul on its journey back to rebirth.

The lightning zone is the first cosmic propositus which activises the process of rebirth. On the event of death, the departed soul may or may not reach this impersonal entity. The decisive factor is the individual account of the actions of the departed soul. The excellent souls may attain an abode with this impersonal entity, or may be detained at any anterior stations in the yonder space, elaborately named in the above order in the *Chhandogya Upnishad*.[2]

It should not be missed that each planet has its own *Samvatsar* and has its own position in the cosmic space.

1. Ibid.
2. 5/10.

Both the tracks are therefore, relative, because they are in relation to the position of the planet.

The North and South are dimensions in relation to the planet, and it is only because of the planet that these dimensions can be contemplated. The North track is relatable to the Sun being in North of the Equator, and, likewise, the South track is the situation of the Sun in the South of the Equator of any particular planet. The truth, however, is that, the Sun does not move, only the planets move. The North and the South solstices are not in relation to the Sun but are in relation to the planet.

The fact that the Sun might have its own motion or its own orbit is a different matter. In relation to the planet, the Sun is stationary. The terms *Uttarayana* and *Dakshiayana* are otherwise related to the signs of the Zodiac. These twelve signs of the Zodiac are configurations of particular constellations which the earth would come across in its revolution round the Sun. Depicted in this way, the North solstice is when the Earth is exposed to the sign of Capricorn in the Zodiac, and, otherwise, that is, the southern solstice is when the Earth is exposed to the Sun while cutting across the constellation of Cancer in the sign of Zodiac. Geographically construed, the *Uttarayana* or the *Devyan* track is open when the earth is exposed to the Sun with the stretch of land within its Tropic of Capricorn whereas the South solstice would be when the exposure of earth towards Sun is in the area within its Tropic of Cancer.

The entity of *Samvatsar* is not only the line of gravitational force but represents also the period of one mundane year, that is, one year of the mortals. The North and the South solstices would comprise each a period of six months of human comprehension.

The second grade lives do not and cannot reach the *Samvatsar*. From the months covered by the South solstice, they rise to the world of the manes, known as the *Pitraloka*, which is the abode of the departed souls of the ancestors of a human being. From this world of the manes, they accelerate their course through the ethereal space to the Moon, that is, the lunar region. The Moon is not only a planet but also a substance which serves as food for the celestial entities; and the word 'food' essentially means something which appeases or satisfies, as when one says that beauty is food of the eyes or music is the food of ears. The virtuous lives having traversed the *Samvatsar*, as also the solar and the lunar peripheries, succeed in getting to the region of the lightning, become immune from rebirths, staying there in perfect peace, which does not mean that they would never become liable to a future birth. In course of time, which can extend to any era, they also return to the mortal world after the merits of their past actions are exhausted. The *Bhagwadgita*[1] states that having enjoyed the heavenly peace, in the sparkling lights, till the balance sheet of actions gets neutralised, and thence, they return to the world of mortals.

The departed soul, voyaging through the cosmic space, whether on the North track or the South track, are both destined to return to the mortal world, the difference being only in the period or the spell of time, and the balance sheet of the actions of the departed soul is automatically worked out by the law of *karma*. Whereas in case of taking the North track, it may take epochs, in case of taking the South track, the return to the mortal world may be matter of years, months or days, and the span of time is commensurate mathematically

1. 9/21.

with the credit balance in the account book of the departed soul.

The virtuous are reborn either in the royal lineage or among the class of erudite scholars. The second grade lives are reborn as good citizens. However, those having no access to either track, are born in the lower order of the brutes.[1] The life on rebirth, cannot be precisely calculated or predicted. The law or *karma* automatically computes it and allots any life to any soul, of course, on the value of the credit balance. It is possible that merit being equal between two souls, they may yet be allotted different lives, and this is in consonance with the plain rule of parity that different things may have equal value. If the rebirth answers the same value in the case of rebirth as an elephant or a horse, or pig or a donkey, any life matching with the account can be allotted.

There is no ban on manufacturing altogetherly a fresh model. There is no chance of groping into the mystic operation of the law of *karma*. What is notable, is that, multiplicity in the species comes about by execution of the fiat of *Karma*. It is notable, again, that this formidable law operates both on macro and micro levels. **There is a collective *Samskara* of the creation as a whole and the next creation is bound to generate the creatures in accordance with the *Samskara* of the last creation. On the micro level, it is calculated and applied on the life of one particular individual. It is the law which decrees afresh in each particular case and there can be no uniform rule specifying the type of life, a soul would live on its rebirth.** What is pith and substance of the rule, is that merit has to be rewarded in its perfect mathematical return. The type or the kind of reward is no consideration. The gravity of the balance sheet is the

1. *Chhandogya Upnishad,* 5/10/7-8.

criteria, and the reward may be X, Y or Z, provided the three are exactly equal in value.

The *Manusmriti*[1] has, of course provided sufficient clues to predict what action would procure what life on rebirth, or, conversely, the state of present life may be because of presumed actions of the past life, but it is after all a guess-work, and the principle of the guess, and not its consequence, is alone accurate. It is indeed a code of conduct teaching a person the way to lead his life. The aim has been to keep the race aware of the law of *karma*.

The law of *karma* is logical mathematics and mathematical logic. The law of *karma* has a premium of reasonableness to its acceptability.

The inevitable conclusion is that the models, types or patterns of life are not virtually evolved but assorted by the law of *karma*.

5. Conclusion

The cosmos is a manufactory of life. The *Veda*[2] has contemplated an impersonal entity which is busy with the art of manufacturing models, types, brands, images or patterns of life. This impersonal entity is named as the *Brahmanspati*, who manufactures all these models at his own will and choice and its choice is dynamic, because it works like a smith active on his bellows. The law of *karma* is the executive machinery of this entity named as *Brahmanspati*. The models and patterns have not evolved but are manipulated in a process where patterns may go on in repetition, where new models might come into existence and the existing ones may become extinct. **The patterns of life are a cosmic phenomenon operated by the law of *karma*, admitting of some arbitrariness but absolutely ruling out any irrationality.**

1. Ch.-12.
2. *Rigveda*, 10/72.

The promenade of the life principle in the cosmic space and the metamorphosis of the life principle into patterns, is not haphazard but proceeds on holistic principle.

CHAPTER 6
PATTERNS OF LIFE

SYNOPSIS

1. *Rishi* as Source of Life
2. Meaning of *Rishi*
3. Precise Conclusions
4. Formation of Life Patterns

1. *Rishi* as Source of Life

It is stated in the *Shatapath Brahmin*, at several places, and reiterated in other *Brahmins*, that the *Rishis* are verily the life. The *Bhagwadgita*[1] elaborates on the same thing, saying:

> "The great seers (*Rishis*), their four elders (*Sanaka* and others) and the fourteen *Manus* or the progenitors of mankind (the *Swayambhuvah* and his thirteen successors) are the mind-born cosmic personalities from whom all other creatures are born."

The seven great *Rishis* are the seven stars composing the *Ursa Major* or the *Great Bear*. The *Manusmriti*[2] refers to ten *Rishis* named as *Marichi, Atri, Angira, Pulastya, Pulah, Kratu, Pracheta, Vasishtha, Bhrigu* and *Narada*. They are regarded as the first mind-born sons of *Brahma*, the Lord Creator. The *Vishnu Purana*[3] while explaining the term *Manu*, has stated that the creator first brought

1. 10/6.
2. 1/35.
3. 1/7/1-19.

about his nine mind-born sons, namely, *Bhrigu, Pulastya, Pulah, Kratu, Angira, Marichi, Daksha, Atri* and *Vasishtha*.

The *Manusmriti*[1] has summarised the same theme, stating:

> "From the *Rishis* were born the *Pitras*, from *Pitras*, the gods and demons, and from the gods, the whole world, mobile and immobile, in due order."

The word *Pitras* denotes the line of ancestry, that is, the manes.

The *Vāyu Purana*[2] describes the seven *Rishis*, as follows:

> "They are seven in number and are possessed of seven virtues. Hence, they are called *Sapt Rishis*. They are long lived and composers of *Vedic Hymns*, possessed of divine powers and transcendent virtues and supreme in merits, learning and age. They are credited with an intuitive or direct perception of the divine law and are the founders of progenies multiplying in families."

These *Rishis* are the agents of creation. The human beings are born from and are progeny of these *Rishis*. In the *Mahabharata*[3] the seven *Rishis* are named as *Marichi, Angira, Atri, Pulastya, Pulah, Kratu,* and *Vasishtha*. The demon King, *Ravana*, is recognised, in scriptures, as the grand-son of *Pulastya*.

In the *Vedic* metaphysics, these *Rishis* are the principalities or the reservoirs of cosmic life.

The constellation of seven stars known as the Great Bear are celestial potentialities or the potentates of cosmic life, and are often designated as *Deva Rishis*. The Pole

1. 3/201.
2. 61/93-94.
3. *Shantiprava*, Ch.-340, 69-70.

Star, gazing straight on the Great Bear, is also a celestial entity named as *Dhruva*, and the seven named *Rishis* are at once watched over by *Dhruva*. It is notable, however, that *Dhruva*, although the Lodestar of the named seven *Rishis*, constituting the Great Bear, is not a *Rishi*. The constituents of Great Bear being stars, **the word '*Rishi*' finally means a Star.**

Dhruva is the one singular star which is static, having no motion of its own. The *Samskrit* word '*Dhruva*' denotes an inertia, a state devoid of motion. The intrinsic motion common to all stars is essentially the life principle. **The alchemy of life is traced to the motion or dynamicity essentially associated with a *Rishi*.** The chemistry of life is worked out from the dynamicity of particular Stars. Life is name of dynamicity. Staticity is death. The concentric motion of the *Rishi* is the generator of life, and life is a continuous ongoing process. In the cosmos, the loss of dynamicity brings about dissolution, and death of a creature as cessation of his activity, operates on the same analogy. The *Veda* has correctly contemplated this state of dissolution as a deep abyss of darkness when there was no life. Life breaks through this abyss of darkness by force of its dynamicity and the universe is at once activised to remain active till the point of dissolution.

The *Vayu Purana*[1] describes the following characteristics of a *Deva Rishi*:

> "Seers living in the celestial regions should be known as the blessed *Deva Rishis*. Besides them, there are other *Deva Rishis* as well who are distinguished by their knowledge of the past, present and future and strict adherence to truth. In other words, celestials, *Brahmins*, and members of

1. 61/88-92.

> the royal classes which are famed throughout the world for their austerity, who have imparted spiritual knowledge to devotees (like *Prahalad*) even in their mother's womb, who are the revealers of *Mantras* or sacred formulas, who by virtue of their supernatural powers (*Siddhi*) have unrestricted access everywhere, and as ever surrounded by *Rishis*, are all *Deva Rishis*."

The *Deva Rishis* are, thus, superior entities having their own followers or disciples or descendants who are subordinate to or under control of a *Deva Rishi*. Like any other *Samskrit* word, the word *'Rishi'* has its own etymological meaning.

2. Meaning of *Rishi*

The word *'Rishi'* is frequent in *Vedic* literature. In the *Samskrit* alphabet, each letter has a full meaning. The word *'Rishi'* is a combination of two words *'Ri'* or *'shi'*. The letter *'Ri'* is a vowel, and the letter *'shi'*, again, is an association of the consonant *'sha'* modified by the vowel *'i'*. The root *'Ri'* stands for equanimity, poise or balance. It is in conformity with the same meaning ascribed to the *Samskrit* word *'Rit'*, which stands for cosmic balance. The cosmos is real. The root *'Ri'* stands also for truth or the state of existence. The vowel *'i'* when pressed upon the root *'Ri'* stands for motion or dynamicity. The root *'sha'* stands for light, and which is again modulated by the vowel *'i'*. This *'i'* stands for wisdom. The word *'Rishi'*, therefore, in its composite form, means a dynamic embodiment of light and learning. Truth, wisdom and motion are the fundamental characteristics of a *Rishi*. The *Rishis* are true because they are self-born. They have inherent motion and the property of their dynamicity follows in a stream of life. They are progenitors and they live as long as their progeny continues.

Since the word *'Rishi'* stands both as source and testimony of life, it verily knows the character, quality and the course of life it is prone to bestow on the mortal world; and this clairvoyance on their part is self-evident.

However, in the mundane sense, the *Rishis* are also persons who maintain a seminary for teaching the disciples and imparting knowledge of cosmic secrets to them.

The synesis of *Samskrit* words is traced from one or the other acoustic unit, called its root or the origin, and each acoustic unit is a pronounced pattern constituted by joining a vowel to some consonant. A consonant is only a flow of air from the lungs which in itself is a mere inaudient exercise and can serve as an audient only when supplied with a vowel. A vowel, hence, becomes capable of becoming an audible sound pattern only with the aid of a vowel. The root of any *Samskrit* word is, therefore, a consonant with its appropriate vowel additive.

The word *'Rishi'* is, however, a duplex of two roots, namely, *Ri* and *shi*. The root *Ri*, as stated above, denotes a balance or uniformity. The root *shi* is again a compound of two roots, namely, *sh* and *i*. The root *sh* stands for light or reflection whereas the root *i* stands for intellect, culminating into some impulse or desire. **Impulse or desire is only intellect activised.**

The word *'Rishi'*, therefore, represents an embodiment of deep meditational power.

The root *Ri* connotes also an action of spinning, in deep meditational reflection. A *Rishi* only spins around his own self, gaining an intuitive firsthand knowledge of truth or being. Since the planets also have a tendency of spinning around their axis, they, in certain *Vedic* references, are also conceived and denominated as *Rishis*.

The *Shatatapa Brahmin* which is a prosified exegetive part of the *Yajurveda,* has synonymised the word *Rishi* with life.

The word *'Rishi'* has, thus, a tertiary blend of meanings, two exoteric and one esoteric. In the exoteric sense, it refers primarily to those persons of intuitive perception who in the preterite past, had perceived the *Vedic Hymns* through which the cosmic secretes were grasped by them as revelations which, in recurring sequence, were handed down, to their descendants or disciples and who establish themselves as institutions of *Vedic* lore recognised, in course of time, as centres of learning for the students and the laity. In the Post-*Vedic* period, the *Rishis* are preachers or proctors in the mundane institutions functioning as seminaries instituted for lessons in *Vedic* philosophy.

In the esoteric sense, the *Rishis,* are principalities of life. They are principles of life, composed as models or archetypes of life. It is through them that the creaturehood on earth is modelled or modulated in a gradual developing order. They are the components of the geneological roots of all creatures generated on earth. They are the original genes in an abstract and unmanifest state, which, in course of natural alchemic processes, culminate into a chromosomal unit enveloping the entire history of heredity or the whole ancestry of any creature.

The *Rishis* can, thus, be taken as particular patrimonial principalities, devolving, in turn, to the *Pitras,* becoming responsible for birth of real mortals. Since the lunar region is believed to be the abode of the *Pitras,* the *Rishis* must be having the solar region as their habitat. The *Rishis* as well as the *Pitras* are both peculiar forms, the latter being a concomitant modification through nature's own agitations. The words 'god' (*deva*), and demon (*danava*) are just terms of art, conceivably versed in the figurative sense, representing, respectively, the virtuous and the vicious, being the two contrasting natures, one, the kind or the gentle, and the other, as cruel or ferocious.

The words 'gods' and 'demons' can well stand respectively for human beings and beasts, and as regards the latter, they can denote the giant sized beasts, like the dinosaur.

If the apocalypse in the *Bible*[1] that 'God created man in his own image', be taken as gospel truth, the word 'god' aptly stands for the human and the semi-human beings. From the *Rishis* to the *Pitras*, and from the *Pitras* to the gods and demons, what is denoted is the descending rounds of births, different from the concept of cycle of rebirth. The *Pitras* falling down in the latter round of generation of divine species or the *deva*, and the demonic species denominated as the *Rakshasa*, at war with each other, thus, depict two distinct orders whereof the latter implies the birth of irresponsible agents of one and the same cosmic law; and there might have been giants in days of yore as is warranted by the evolutionary series in the biological world, since in the lower biological order, there is evidence of the same in the flora, going *pari passu* with the fauna in respect of their size and behaviour, yielding a clue that the pretty diminutive ferns are the descendants of the gigantic ferns which must have grown in the carboniferous age, and, likewise, the giant beastly demons might have been descendants of the *Pitras* in the Jurassic age.

Each *Rishi* or each *Pitra* is a propositus, having its own progeny. The *Vayu Purana*[2] has described the lineal descendency, of the *Rishis* and the *Pitras* consisting of

---

1. *Genesis*, 1/27.
2. *See* Ch.-28-30.

thousands of sons and, then thousands of grand-sons and so on.

The *Manusmriti*[1] holds that the various groups or families of ancestors are the sons of all the *Rishis* headed by *Marichi* and other seers who are mind-born sons of *Manu*, the self-born. The *Manusmriti*[2] than proceeds to describe the various types of *Pitras*. The *Somasads* are sons of *Viraja*, known as the ancestors of the *Sadhyas*, *Agnishvatta*, who are sons of *Marichi*, are considered to be the ancestors of gods. The *Barhishad* are said to be sons of *Atri*, recognised as the ancestors of *Daityas*, *Danavas*, *Yakshas*, *Gandharvas*, *Serpents*, *Rakshasas*, *Suparnas*, that is the winged creatures. and *Kinnaras* representing the race of eunuchs. The *Pitras* of *Brahmins* are *Somapas*, that is, who drink *Soma*. The *Pitras* of *Kshatriyas* are *Havirbhuja*, that is, who feed on the oblations offered in the sacred-fire, the *Pitras* of *Vaishyas* are *Ajyapas*, that is, who feed on soft and greasy substances like butter. The *Pitras* of *Shoodras* are *Sukalins*, who survive only with the time, time being their only sustenance. Again, *Somapas* are sons of *Kavya*, who survive on cooked food. The *Havishmantas*, which survive, again, on the food offered to fire, are sons of *Angira*. The *Ajyapas* are sons of *Pulastya*. The *Sukalins* are sons of *Vashishtha*. The *Anagnidagdhas*, whom the fire cannot burn, the *Agnidagdha* whom the fire can burn, the *Kavya*, who feed on cooked food, *Barhishads*, who sit on grass or mat, since the word *'Barhi'* means grass, who also accept oblations of cooked food, the *Agnishvattas*, who feed on offerings made to the fire, and *Saumyas*, who are gentle chaste and perfectly pure, are all regarded as ancestors only of the *Brahmins*. It must be understood, however, that these are just principal classes

---

1. 1/34-35.
2. 3/195-201.

of ancestors who would have countless sons and grandsons.

The birth of men and beasts, metaphorically taken as the gods and the demons, from the manes, and that of manes themselves from *Rishis,* furnishes an account only of the transition of spirit; and this is so because the *Rishis* or even the *Pitras,* cannot be conceived of as having carnal bodies, yet they have bodies in the sense only of a linear configuration. They must have ethereal, auric or astral bodies, since without attributing them with bodies, it would have been futile to endow them with specific names. The super-eminent name, endowed to a particular *Rishi,* virtually denotes its peculiar brand of the life principle, which is, in itself, an assemblage of several subservient life principles in compact kinship, as if it was a group, consisting of or composed as a gamut, burgeoning into its own ramifications simulating the membership in a compact family, preserving its original brand or archetype in its onward transition into the manifest carnal life of creatures.

The creatures being an embodiment both of spirit and a carnal frame, it was natural for the interpreters to account not only for the spiritual but also for their carnal ancestry. The carnal mass in the life of a creature is, likewise, traced to a line also of its material ancestry.

The following statement of *Manusmriti*[1] has given a due share, in the line of ancestry, also to the material particles coinciding in the composition of the physical frames of the creatures:

> "The fathers, they say, are the *Vasus,* the grandfathers are the *Rudras* and the great-grand-fathers are the *Aadityas,* such is an ancient scriptural statement."

1. 3/284.

What is relevant is the propositus and the phyla, that is, the branches or dynasties of any particular *Rishi* or *Pitra,* having significance only from point of view of nomenclature of different phyla. What is significant is that the *Pitras* are born from a *Rishi,* and each *Rishi* can have numerous phyla of its own, and the origin of a particular branch of humanity has to be ascribed to a particular *Rishi.* Down in the line of ancestry representing the pater families are the *Vasus,* counted in number to be eight, namely, the fire, the earth, the air, the *Antariksha,* which is a term for the atmospheric space in general, then, the *Aadityas,* roughly taken to be the Sun but metaphysically conceived as the solar months, the *Dyau,* a term denoting the blaze or radiance, the Moon and the *Nakshatras* or the *asterisms* in the path of the Moon comprising between twenty-seven and twenty-eight Stars. The term *Vasudha,* which is a term representing the geographical globe, literally means the earth which is the bearer of all these forces, and has been derived from the term *Vasu.* The *Pitras* being the ancestors of men, and the *Rishis* being the progenitors of the *Pitras,* the origin of any man is traced to a particular *Rishi.*

The grand paternalism is endowed to the *Rudras,* which are eleven forms or modifications or operations of one and the same life breath, named, in respect of each of its eleven exertions, as the *Pran, Apan, Vyan, Samana, Udan, Nag, Koorma, Krikal, Devdutta, Dhananjaya* and the eleventh being the main life spark, commonly understood as the *Jeevatma* or the soul proper, which is the main spiritual content of life, distinct from the physical frame. All these eleven are controllers of the life force vibrating at different levels of the body.

The *Aadityas* is plural of the term *Aaditya,* conceived as the Sun, with its plurality representing the twelve months in the cycle of the whole year, and are conceived to be the great-grand-fathers. This way, **the life principle is traced to the solar energy.**

These thirty-one, are, then, united with *Indra*, which is a name given independently to the electrical energy of the Sun, and with the *Prajapati* or the Auriga, which is the aurora representing the bands of light, some time seen in the sky in the polar regions. The word '*Prajapati*' is the proverbial name for the main progenitor, the deemed creator. All these have been counted in the *Rigveda*[1] and in the *Yajurveda*[2] as also in the *Atharva Veda*[3], as the thirty-three basic divinities, combining to compose the physical frame of any creature and responsible for the control and composure of a creature's body as a whole. All these are chemical and the physical ingredients of the body of a creature.

Life is not spirit alone or matter alone, but an inherence of spirit into a material frame. The composition of life has inevitably a double or two-fold ancestry, the spiritual as well as the material. The spiritual ancestry is associated with the *Rishi* through a particular *Pitra*; and the other thirty-one, as named above, are the physical constituents of life. What can be logically deduced from the above account, is that the *Rishis* and the *Pitras*, and, likewise, the gods and the demons, each being antecedent and devolving into its consequents, form a continuous chain responsible for the entire biogenesis, and though not living beings, they are yet live entities or active agents in the phenomena of life.

The term 'life' as literally interpreted is only a state of being alive, but the word 'alive' is itself susceptible to a

1. 6/2/35/1.
2. 14/31.
3. 10/23/4/23, 27.

double implication, exoteric as well as esoteric. Being alive exoterically refers to a state of *de facto* living, but when conceived esoterically, it stands for the potentiality or verve for springing into life. It is the esoteric cause leading to an exoteric effect as, corroborated by the *Samkhya* philosophy, that the cause is more real than the effect.

The tree is alive in the seed because the tree potentially exists in its seed. The seed unless deformed, damaged or destroyed, continues to be all alive because when thrown into the womb of the earth, it is destined to sprout out and become, in course of time, a full dress tree. The trunk, the twigs and the tendons, all, are potentially existent in the seed, and in nothing else than the seed. **The seed is alive from which the tree has come out to be a living thing.**

The above exegesis of the concept of *Rishi*, inevitably, leads to certain conclusions, not only approximately accurate but also precisely exact.

3. Precise Conclusions

Each biological proclivity must have a seed, which, in the abstract sense, is an impetus or inspiration to ooze out into real life, floral, faunal or human. The enigma is that the seed comes from a tree and the tree comes again from the seed. The enigma having no dogmatic answer, the inquisition, involving its logical answer, can only be that there has to be the seed of the seed itself. The seed must trace its own origin. The seed is itself an incarnation materialized from some idea, some principle, or some impression transcendental to the seed.

There is no indication writ anywhere in the seed to foretell the shape or the size of the tree, yet the magnitude and the ramification of the tree are all latent in the seed which is just a tiny chrysalis equalling a grain.

The seed is only the embodiment of a principle inherent and immanent therein. The seed is itself a material encasement of a transcendental principle, a subtle, abstract law, existing apart from and independent of the seed. **The seed is just a tiny embodiment of some elemental concentrate elsewhere in space but congealed into the seed by nature's own alchemy.**

The elemental concentrate of the seed trickles down by incident of nature, from higher space, on to the earth, traversing several processes of nature, and gets fertilized and gestated in the womb of the earth, sprouts out, grows and develops, in course of time, into a tree, which then starts begetting its own seeds. The latent principle in the seed becomes a patent presentation, and the process continues recurrently.

That manifest comes from the unmanifest, is the secretive theme of creation. That patent comes from the latent, is the perennial law. The seed is only an embodied capsule of its latent principle which is real, ideational specimen or pattern of life concentrate. **The curious *Vedic* term *Rishi* connotes these latent abstract life concentrates, responsible both for** biogenesis and biometrics. As an ouija of biometric substantialities, they are innumerable, though scriptures have undertaken to name them as emblems of particular lives, such as *Bhrigu, Angira, Atri, Vashishtha, Matsya, Agastya, Pulastya, Pulah, Kritu, Marichi, Sanaka, Prachetas, Narada, Parvat, Ayasya, Ghor, Shunak, Pragath, Atharva, Bharadwaj, Gautam, Jamadagni, Vishvamitra, Kashyapa, Shanyu, Kantha, Kaushik, Gritsmad,* and many others, outlisting any catalogue of names, contemplated in the *Purana* literature. As principalities of cosmic life, these names signify numerous brands and branches of life and need not be confused with the *sages* or *saints* born as mortal personages bearing identical names. The *Mahabharata*[1] has for convenience, shortlisted them, explaining that they are *Prakriti* or modes of life, signifying the oncoming currents in the reservoir of life, and it is as futile to go by their names as to undertake an exercise of counting all the possible species of flora and fauna. **The *Rishis* are primal seeds of life.** The manes or the *Pitras* are later secretions of the *Rishis*, and, then, the entities conceived as the gods and demons, is a derivative, saturated in further process, from the *Pitras*; and it is in this sense that the *Manusmriti*[2] described the *Pitras* as born of *Rishis*, and the gods and demons, from the *Pitras*, and lastly, all things mobile and immobile from the gods and the demons. As all diversity comes about from a unity, all *Rishis*, as multiform life principles, are, as they must be, issued forth from one monistic life principle, and since all life on earth has its origin from the solar principle, the *Shwetashwaropnishad*[3] accepts the Sun as one original *Rishi*, and all species are explained as the offsprings of Sun, named in that *Upnishad* as the *Kapil Rishi*. *Kapil* literally means *auric*, yellow or golden, the Sun is named as *Kapil* because of its *auric* radiance.

Whether *Rishis* or *Pitras*, the scriptures believe that they do not exist as isolated units but constitute each a family of innumerable *Kindred*, capable of commuting and permuting *inter se*, identified in scriptures through archaic but complacent nomenclatures with little cosmological significance but employed more as an aid to their intelligibility. The process is a downward order of the life principle leading their implicit features to gradually become explicit fabrications into positive

---

1. *Shantiprava*, Ch.-340.
2. 3/201.
3. 5/2.

patterns impelled to develop and exhibit concrete configurations.

The formation of these primal seeds, hithertofore referred as life patterns, is nature's own alchemy.

4. Formation of Life Patterns

An insight into the formation of the life patterns on cosmic canvas can be the sole clue to explaining these myriads of creaturehood on earth. The process of becoming manifest from the unmanifest is the eternal cosmogenic tantrism, and the preliminaries are sheerly simplistic. The *Vedic* philosophy has traced this manifestation into a duality of spirit and matter which in the *Vedic* terminology are synonymized as the *Purusha* and the *Prakriti.*

Whereas the *Purusha* is immutable, the *Prakriti* is dynamic principle subject to further morphogenesis. In the first phase, the *Prakriti* unfolds itself in the form of boundless space, called the *aakash,* known as the firsthand evolute of the *Prakriti,* and, then, the air, the fire, the water and, finally, the earth are the consequent derivative evolutes, each antecedent evolute being inherent in its consequents, and all forming a unified whole, and, each, taken distinctly, are called the *Bhoota,* but taken cumulatively, they are called the *Panchmahabhuta,* or the five primordial elements considered as the material cause of anything mobile and immobile, the animate and the inanimate, the creatures and objects, and all and everything.

Any material cause, as science asserts, can be traced to its atomic content, and the difference of one from another thing is the amassive arrangement of atoms, better expressed in cosmological terms as cosmotrons. The *Samskrit* word *Trasarenu* is conceivably the exact equivalent of a cosmotron. The fleck of dust seen when the light of Sun is seen reflected through a lattice, is called *Trasarenu*[1]. The motive force of the cosmotrons is what the cosmos fundamentally and finally stands for. The cosmotrons considered as the basal content of this mysterious universe are instrumental in maintaining the constant flow of force in the form of violent motion. An embodied entity cannot be anything different from a given mass of electronically charged cosmotrons, cavorting in a state of formidable motion; and the difference, diversity or variance between embodied entities is an output of the variance in the force of that motion. The sound which is the essential inalienable attribute of the *aakash*, with the aid of cosmic light, is responsible for the constancy of this motion. The light and sound, inhering in each other, correspond only to the different whorls of agitation in the basal substance with no inherent change in the substance. **The dissimilarity in the whorls caused by such agitation explains the difference in the appearance of things.**

The manifest world as a whole, is an immense eternal motion. The miscellany perceptible in the universe is the cognation in proportion with the quantum and periodicity of that motion, be it the cosmos as a whole or a thing in isolation.

The variegated appearance of a thing occurring to any human being depends on how he feels or is able to perceive or grasp the floating waves generated by the whorling motion of cosmotrons, the tendency of which is to resolve the material universe into the wave patterns.

Sir James Jeans, in his *Mysterious Universe* holds that physics finally resolves the material universe into waves and nothing but waves. For a better result, this proposition can be modified by construing these waves as wave patterns, more explicitly, the cosmotronic pattern.

---

1. *Manusmriti*, 8/132.

The cosmotrons are only tiny imperceptible particles of star dust. These grains of the star dust, in their revolving motion, collide with and stick to each other, due to their electrical attraction liable to form linear diagrams.

These diagrams being allotropic or allomorphic, their tendency to run into myriads, is automatic and inevitable, without any extrinsic intervention, and a chance of similarity, dissimilarity, identity, similitude or contrast is part of the cosmic game, for the plain reason that the roving revolution of the particles goes in rounds and numbers which can never be uniform because of their inherent difference in attrition and attraction, repulsion and reluctance, at times higher and heavier while at others lower or lighter gravitational pushes and pulls, yielding infinite varieties in the resultant patterns.

These patterns being some configurative arrangement of cosmotrons are sort of subtle diagrammatic impressions, replicating in the imagery of bodies of astral, aural or ethereal content strewn abruptly on the canvas of cosmic space, prone and liable, in due course to develop into corresponding physical frames of gross matter.

The area surrounding an animate body, is itself evidence of the given pattern ingesting and yet outglowing the given body. All bodies are surrounded with this aural radiance which is an imponderable fluid. The aura though one of the unrevealed secrete of the ancient cabala, is just the emanation of the outcoming glow of the pattern imbedded in the body. The pattern is deposited and encased in the body and yet transcends and mysteriously surrounds it in the form of its aura.

There is then a whole genera of such patterns which are in a continuous process of making, unmaking and remaking.

The stars, planets and galaxies in different shapes and sizes are accretions of gross matter amassed layer after layer on their intrinsic pattern, and the residuum of the stardust not metamorphosed into lump of solid corpus, remains swarming in their roving whirl in the space, forming, reforming and deforming themselves into diagrammatic patterns or modalities, which serve as the cynosures of life; and the denomination of *Rishis* connotes only this pseudomorphic prodigy of nature.

When planets have been formed, these patterns or cynosures of life, trickledown by their own magnetic force in the first phase to the lunar region where they are coated upon by sort of secretive sap, commonly known in the *Vedic* science as the *Soma*, and the *Rishis* become the *Pitras*; and the auric patterns assume an astral body. The accretive action of the *Soma* furnishes these bodies with respective organs and senses. These bodies are tenuous miniature capsules.

Again, by magnetic interaction between the Moon and the Earth, these patterns trickle down, in the next phase, down to the earth, in the same way as a sperm makes its way into an ovum of a primiparous mother. The mother earth, after completing its due gestational process, then, issues forth a compact body in its epicenic form, which, by its own aphrodisiac pull, bifurcates itself into two that is, into the male and the female counterparts, and the later process, follows from seed to seed through the art of mating. The original pattern of life thereafter gets deposited into the seminal fluid of the male counterpart, sown by cohabitation into the ovum of the female counterpart, and the genetic process continues in a facile way eventuating both an ethnic progeny and erotic pleasure.

The auric bodies of the *Rishis* by this process gets encased in the sheath of a mortal frame in order to maintain the perennial procreative process, and are relegated unto the *Pitras* or the *Rishis*, after the physical death of a living being.

The *Vedic* ethology has its own themes, introducing a terse principle of the law of *karma*, as to on what merit a departed soul could traverse back to its *Rishidom* or *Pitrahood*, or, when lacking in merit, not capable to reach even the abode of the *Pitras*, doomed to hover around the biosphere, destined to descend down soon to be reborn as brute or other ignoble or despicable species or, in their last disdained destiny, to sprout out as the mute and immobile vegetative species; and, of course, it is a vast subject having its own technicalities.

That the vegetal species still linger in their hermaphrodite state carries again, its cosmic purpose because they serve as the foodstuff for the animal beings. It is through the consumption of the vegetative stuff that the seminal fluid as the sole procreative agent is secreted after a number of processes which the digested food had undergone, and without the secretion of which no procreative process could have been realised, though it cannot be doubted that the first of any vegetative species must have come through the same process of their parent patterns inseminated from space into the womb of the earth.

The *Bhagwadgita*[1], the *Manusmriti*[2] and the *Chhandogya Upnishad*[3], have explained the vegetative stuff as the sap of life, in their own context, but agreeing on fundamentals. The *Brihadaranyak Upnishad*[4] has aptly compared the male and the female counterparts with a corn of the seed which is a compact union of its two

1. 3/14.
2. 3/76.
3. 1/1/2.
4. 1/4/3.

halves joined together by an occluding seam, and these two halves serve in relation to the flora, the same purpose as the male and the female counterparts; and the tree then begets its own seed.

The life patterns retained in the seed dropped into water, become aquatic species, and those deposited into the bosom of the earth make out a multitude of creaturehood. The process of avian species is not different and the laying of their eggs on the earth is evidence that they are begotten by and from the earth.

The species carryout the purpose and policy of creation. The patterns of life, in their incognito and incorporeal configurations, stay in the space, creating and recreating themselves, so that the genesis of a new life pattern in the space becomes the replica for any new species on earth and a chance cessation of any form in the domain of *Rishis* must be followed by the evanescence of its corresponding species on the earth. **The physical biodiversity on earth is consequence of metaphysical abiogenesis.**

SUBJECT INDEX

O

P

•••